WRITERS AND THEIR WORK

ISOBEL ARMSTRONG
General Editor

OSCAR WILDE

OSCAR WILDE

Alexandra Warwick

NORTHCOTE

BRITISH COUNCIL

ATLANTIC
PUBLISHERS & DISTRIBUTORS (P) LTD

For Stephen, Kerri and Em

This edition is published by
ATLANTIC
PUBLISHERS & DISTRIBUTORS (P) LTD
7/22, Ansari Road, Darya Ganj, New Delhi-110 002
Tel: 40775252, 23273880, 23275880, 23280451; Fax: +91-11-23285873
E-mail: orders@atlanticbooks.com; Web: www.atlanticbooks.com

By arrangement with
Northcote House Publishers Ltd
Horndon House, Horndon, Tavistock, Devon, PL19 9NQ,
United Kingdom. (T)+44(0)1822 810066; (F)+44(0)1822 810034
(E) northcote.house@virgin.net and (W) www.northcotehouse.co.uk
The *Writers and their Work* series is published in association with the British Council.

First Indian Reprint 2010
First published in 2007 by Northcote House Publishers Ltd

ISBN 978-81-269-1291-9

British Library Cataloguing-in-Publication Data
A catalogue record for this book is available from the British Library

Typeset by TW Typesetting, Plymouth, Devon
Printed in India at Nice Printing Press, A-33/3A, Site-IV, Industrial Area, Sahibabad, Ghaziabad, U.P.

Contents

Acknowledgements

With thanks for this, as for so much else, to David Cunningham and Leigh Wilson. And to those who, in their different ways, helped me to write it: Isobel Armstrong, Bill Batten, Mark Currie, Sondeep Kandola, Kirsten Heckterman and Izzie Thomas.

Biographical Outline

1854 Oscar Fingal O'Flahertie Wills Wilde born in Westland Row, Dublin, on 16 October, second child of Jane and William Wilde.

1855 Family moves to Merrion Square, Dublin.

1864–71 Portora Royal School, Enniskillen.

1867 Death of sister Isola, aged 9.

1871–4 Enters Trinity College, Dublin, with a scholarship. Taught by J. P. Mahaffy.

1874 Enters Magdalen College Oxford with a scholarship.

1876 Death of father, William Wilde.

1877 Visits Greece and Rome with Mahaffy.

1878 Wins Newdigate Prize for 'Ravenna'. Graduates with First Class degree in Literae Humaniores (Greats).

1879 August: moves to London. Takes an apartment in Salisbury Street with Frank Miles.

1880 *Vera, Or the Nihilists* published privately. Moves with Miles to Keats House, Tite Street, Chelsea.

1881 *Poems* published. Wilde obliged to leave Tite Street after objections from Miles's father to *Poems*. *Vera* withdrawn from planned performance.

1882 Extensive lecture tour of USA and Canada.

1883 February–May: in Paris. Writes *The Duchess of Padua*. August to September: in USA for *Vera*. November: becomes engaged to Constance Lloyd.

1884 May: marries Constance in London. Spends honeymoon in Paris and Dieppe.

1885 January: moves to 16 Tite Street with Constance. May: 'The Truth of Masks' published in the *Nineteenth Century*. 5 June: son Cyril born.

1886 Meets Robert Ross. 5 November: birth of son Vyvyan.

1887 'The Canterville Ghost', 'The Sphinx without a Secret', 'Lord Arthur Savile's Crime' and 'The Model Millionaire' published. November: becomes editor of the *Woman's World*.

1888 May: publication of *The Happy Prince and Other Tales*. 'The Young King' published.

1889 January: 'The Decay of Lying' published in the *Nineteenth Century*; 'Pen, Pencil and Poison' in *Fortnightly Review*; 'The Portrait of Mr W.H.' in *Blackwood's Magazine*. October: ceases editing the *Woman's World*.

1890 *The Picture of Dorian Gray* published in *Lippincott's Magazine*; 'The Critic as Artist' in two parts, the July and August issues of *The Nineteenth Century*.

1891 Meets Lord Alfred Douglas. Publishes 'The Soul of Man under Socialism', *Lord Arthur Savile's Crime and Other Stories, A House of Pomegranates* and *Intentions*. Writes *Salome* in Paris.

1892 *Lady Windermere's Fan* opens. *Salome* banned by the Lord Chamberlain.

1893 *Salome* published in French. *A Woman of No Importance* opens. *Lady Windermere's Fan* published.

1894 *Salome* published in English. 'The Sphinx' and *A Woman of No Importance* published. Visits Florence with Alfred Douglas.

1895 3 January: *An Ideal Husband* opens. 14 February: *The Importance of Being Earnest* opens. 28 February: receives Marquess of Queensberry's card and applies for an arrest for libel. 3 April: first trial opens with Wilde as plaintiff. 5 April: Queensberry acquitted and Wilde arrested. 24 April: creditors force sale of contents of Tite Street house. 29 April: second trial opens with Wilde the defendant on seven counts of gross indecency. 1 May: jury disagree and new trial ordered. 7 May: released on bail. 22 May: third trial opens. 25 May: Wilde sentenced to two years' imprisonment with hard labour; taken from Newgate to Pentonville prison. July: transferred to Wandsworth prison. November: declared bankrupt; moved to Reading prison.

1896 Death of mother, Lady Wilde. 19 February: sees Constance for the last time. *Salome* produced in Paris.

1897 Writes *De Profundis*. 18 May: released and goes straight to Dieppe. May: moves to Berneval-sur-Mer. September: meets Douglas in Naples.

1898 February: leaves Naples for Paris; moves into the Hotel d'Alsace. *The Ballad of Reading Gaol* published. April: death of Constance. Moves about France.

1899 Moves about France, Switzerland and Italy before returning to the Hotel d'Alsace. *The Importance of Being Earnest* published. *An Ideal Husband* published.

1900 October: operation on ear. 30 November: dies in the Hotel d'Alsace; converts to Catholicism on his death-bed. 3 December: buried at Bagneux cemetery.

Abbreviations and References

CW	*Collins Complete Works of Oscar Wilde* (Glasgow: Harper Collins, 2003)
E.	Richard Ellmann, *Oscar Wilde* (London: Hamish Hamilton, 1987)
EL	Oscar Wilde, *Essays and Lectures*, ed. Robert Ross (London: Methuen, 1909)
L.	Merlin Holland and Rupert Hart-Davis, *The Complete Letters of Oscar Wilde* (London: Fourth Estate, 2000)
NB	Philip E. Smith and Michael S. Helfand (eds.), *Oscar Wilde's Oxford Notebooks: A Portrait of a Mind in the Making* (Oxford: Oxford University Press, 1989)

The texts of Wilde's work exist in numerous different versions, and there is still a good deal of debate about the accuracy and authority of some of these versions. Oxford University Press is in the process of producing what will become the standard texts, but as yet only one volume has appeared. For ease of reference I have used the *Collins Complete Works* throughout, but in the Bibliography I have given the first book versions of the individual works as well as the modern editions that are considered most reliable.

Prologue: Situating Wilde

Queen Victoria died on 22 January 1901, surviving by only three weeks the century so closely associated with her. As the beginning of the twentieth century had been widely celebrated on 1 January 1901, her life seemed symbolic in its end, representing for some the regretted passing of a great age and for others the awaited necessary break from a time grown stagnant in which they were impatient for the new. Victoria's death was marked with national mourning. At the funeral five kings followed her coffin through the streets lined with crowds dressed in black. She was buried in the chapel at Frogmore, next to Albert, under the figures of themselves on the tomb, only one of the countless memorials that followed.

Two months earlier, on 30 November 1900, in the last days of the old century, Oscar Wilde died in poverty in a hotel room in Paris. His cheap funeral was attended by a small number of mourners and he was buried in a simple grave in Bagneux cemetery. His obituary in *The Times* was one paragraph, beneath that of a German army officer, and he remained without a public memorial until the centenary of his birth in 1954, when a plaque was placed on his house in Tite Street, Chelsea.

As much as Victoria's death might be thought to be appropriately and neatly placed at the close of the century, the popular conception of Wilde's life and death is the opposite. Although he said of himself, 'I will never outlive the century. The English people will not stand for it' (E. 545), he is now more frequently thought of as a man born into the wrong time, a heroic but ultimately doomed castaway in an unsympathetic age, the very definition of the 'other Victorian' set against the repressive forces of a period, like its queen, for the most part not amused. Richard Ellmann says in his 1987 biography of Wilde that 'he belongs to our world more than Victoria's' (E. 553), and even in 1951 St John Ervine wrote of 'Oscar Wilde, whose life was spent in the Victorian age, a fact sufficiently paradoxical in itself to satisfy even his passion for absurd conjunctions'.[1] It seems that we, to generalize the inhabitants of the later twentieth and early twenty-first centuries, have recognized Wilde as belonging to us: as a creature of modernity, a political radical, a literary innovator, a post-colonial subversive and the inauguarator of queer identity. But, as is always the case with the tempting periodization or the easy opposition of figures like Wilde and Queen Victoria, the elegant symmetry is untrue, and our recognition of Wilde is often a misrecognition, one that says more about what we want to think about our own progress and about our own superiority to the Victorians who would imprison a man for a crime that no longer exists.

It is interesting that, far closer to Wilde's own time, Arthur Ransome, writing in 1912, was able to suggest a rather more complicated relation of the writer and his age. Attempting a critical study of Wilde, he said, 'It is characteristic of great men that, born out of their time, they should come to represent it'[2] – an observation that comes much closer to Wilde's own in *De Profundis*: 'I was a man who stood in symbolic relations to the art and culture of my age' (*CW* 1024). As Ransome presciently suggests, Wilde has come both to represent his time and to be seen as apart from it; he is placed simultaneously in a nostalgia for the exotic *fin de siècle*, as a martyr to Victorian inhumanity and as an iconoclastic Modernist. All these images of Wilde are both true and false, because it is precisely the question of the nature of the symbolic relations in which he stood that has occupied readers of Wilde for a century, and it is the complexity of those relations that makes Wilde a figure of seemingly perpetual interest. As a friend of Wilde's remarked some years after his death, 'the real Oscar Wilde has faded and has been replaced by a strange simulacrum, half invented by the curious, half dictated by the man himself'.[3]

Wilde's notoriously unreliable friend[4] Frank Harris claimed that Wilde told him that 'fifty or a hundred years hence . . . my comedies and my stories and *The Ballad of Reading Gaol* will be read by millions, and even my unhappy fate will call forth world-wide sympathy',[5] but his characteristic sense of his place in history appears to have been far more pessimistic. Especially, and perhaps unsurprisingly, towards the end of his life he expected to be seen as occupying a place somewhere between Gilles de Retz and the Marquis de Sade (*CW* 986). Although there is a general view that after his conviction he was both unspeakable and unspoken of for some seventy years, this is not really the case; the romantic martyr waited a surprisingly short time for his rehabilitation. Wilde's name was removed from the theatre placards for *An Ideal Husband* and *The Importance of Being Earnest*, which were playing at the time of his arrest in 1895, and both plays closed very soon after his conviction. *Earnest* and *Lady Windermere's Fan* were both revived by George Alexander in 1901. Between then and 1914 at least one of his plays was performed almost every year in a major London theatre. Indeed, one of the reviewers of the 1901 revival commented that, on the first night of *Lady Windermere's Fan*, 'there was celebrated a feast of absolution, and, to a certain extent, of rehabilitation'.[6] *The Ballad of Reading Gaol* was published after Wilde's release from prison in 1898, as were the texts of *Earnest* and *Ideal Husband*, and, though the author of the *Ballad* appeared as C.3.3 (his prison number) and *Earnest* as 'the author of *Lady Windermere's Fan*', the veil of anonymity was rather thin. Even as early as 1906, only ten years after the trials,[7] an article appeared in the *Westminster Review* entitled 'The Literary Position of Oscar Wilde', in which the writer, W. L. Leadman, felt able to state:

> The hasty verdict of a rather superficial morality said then that his influence must have been essentially unhealthy . . . we are nce more allowed to discuss Wilde's book without hearing a shocked 'hush' or being suspected of loose views on moral matters. Those who see 'an undercurrent of nasty suggestion' in some of his literary productions must surely be so obsessed by their knowledge of his unfortunate behaviour as to lose all power of disconnecting two absolutely independent things, namely, his art and his private life.[8]

Leadman managed neatly to offer some criticism of Wilde's treatment while at the same time prudently suggesting that there were more interesting things to be said about his career as a writer than as a man convicted of sexual offences. Arthur Ransome's 1912 book also attempted to separate the life of Wilde from his work and was highly circumspect about the events of his life, though Ransome seems to have been the first to suggest the still highly contested idea that Wilde's death was from syphilis, an idea that is repeated by Frank Harris and that forms a central thesis in Ellmann's biography. The line of treating the work rather than the life is the strategy of other mid-twentieth-century major studies, by Edouard Roditi (1947), George Woodcock (1949) and St John Ervine in 1951, and throughout this time editions of his writings continued to appear.[9]

The caution of these earlier critics indicates something of the 'problem' of the linking of Wilde's life and work. At the centre of the dilemma about how to write on Wilde is the issue that occupies much of his own work – the relationship between art and life. The painter Basil Hallward in *The Picture of Dorian Gray* says that 'an artist should create beautiful things, but should put nothing of his own life into them. We live in an age when men treat art as if it were meant to be a form of autobiography' (*CW* 25). As is so often the case with Wilde's writing, Hallward's statement reads as both an invitation and a denial, and much of *Dorian Gray* is in fact concerned with the terrible consequences of an artist's failure to keep his life out of his art. It could be argued that no other author has been so subject to the desire to interpret his life through his writings and vice versa, and it is certainly true that no other British author has suffered such dreadful consequences of this being done. In the trials the prosecution made little distinction between fiction, criticism, letters and actions, and Wilde's attempts to explain the nature of art made no impact: his art was straightforwardly read as autobiography in the most damning fashion.

In the early years of the twentieth century there were a surprising number of biographies and memoirs, many of them driven by the rivalries of those who had been close to Wilde and were endeavouring to establish their version of his story.

Notable among these are the interventions of Lord Alfred Douglas, who wrote several accounts of his own life and of Wilde's, changing his attitude in each of them, but coming in his last version to a more generous assessment of Wilde than he had previously. On the other side were Robert Ross, Robert Sherard and Frank Harris; Ada Leverson, Charles Ricketts and André Gide also produced short (and in Gide's case controversial) recollections. After the deaths of those who had known Wilde, the first significant biography was Hesketh Pearson's in 1946, but by the 1960s the modern Wilde industry had begun in earnest. There were two elements in the renewed attention. The first was a revival of the Victorian *fin de siècle* in fashion and decoration. This was a self-conscious adoption of a decadent counter-cultural style by a new generation of those who saw themselves living for beauty, freedom and progressive ideals in a society that disapproved. Wilde was the principal figure of this view of the *fin de siècle*; he was seen as the king of the decadent Nineties, though the image of the Nineties was itself largely a fabrication established through Holbrook Jackson's *The Eighteen Nineties* (1913) and Richard Le Gallienne's *The Romantic Nineties* (1926). Yeats's introduction to the *Oxford Book of Modern Verse* in 1936 recognized the self-conscious characterization of the period. Observing the change of style in poetry and poets, he wrote 'in 1900 everybody got down off his stilts; henceforth nobody drank absinthe with his black coffee; nobody went mad; nobody committed suicide; nobody joined the Catholic Church; or if they did I have forgotten'.[10]

The second element in the Wilde revival was linked to the very public debates about sexuality that occupied the 1950s and the 1960s. Second-wave feminists were voicing demands for sexual self-determination for women, and there was agitation for homosexual rights. Lord Wolfenden was appointed to head the Committee on Homosexual Offences and Prostitution, and the report from this committee was published in 1957. Wolfenden's report contained a recommendation of the decriminalization of homosexuality, but there was a long delay between the report and the very modified legislation that was finally passed in 1967, which effectively established a male homosexual age of consent at 21. During the many debates

Wilde was frequently cited, both by the softer reformers who presented him as a great writer ruined by harsh and now outdated moral views, and by the more radical campaigners who claimed him as the first of the martyrs in their long persecution. In this sympathetic climate Wilde's son Vyvyan Holland published his memoir of his father, Rupert Hart-Davis edited a selection of letters and H. Montgomery Hyde produced an account of the trials. In 1960 two films dramatizing Wilde's life were released, starring the very well-known actors Robert Morley and Peter Finch. The films were X-rated, restricting their viewing to those over 18, but both gained a great deal of attention, and Finch gathered a Best Actor award for his performance.

Since the 1960s there has been a steady expansion in the Wilde industry and a new reintegration of his life and writings through the critical discourses of gender studies, queer theory, post-colonialism and postmodernism. After his conviction, the *Echo* advised that 'the best thing for everybody now is to forget all about Oscar Wilde, his perpetual posings, his aesthetical teachings and his theatrical productions. Let him go into silence and be heard no more.'[11] The opposite has happened: Wilde has certainly not gone into silence. This is probably a situation of which he would have approved; after all, it was Wilde who observed that the one thing worse than being talked about was not being talked about. A great deal has been said about Wilde, and he said a great deal for and about himself; like the apocryphal American who complained that *Hamlet* was full of quotations, so too is Wilde. Many of his phrases are now part of the common stock, there is a sense of familiarity about him, even of personal acquaintance, and he is frequently cited in lists of historical figures at fantasy dinner parties. Even otherwise sober academic critics fall into the unscholarly temptation to refer to him familiarly as 'Oscar', and this sense of personal investment makes it quite difficult to write about him; it is as though he is already thoroughly known and welcomed as a friend and contemporary. In this book I shall try to show a less familiar Wilde and suggest that he is not always the modern figure that he has been seen as.

Wilde's was a relatively short career and he produced quite a small body of work. Although he is probably best remembered for his society comedies, he moved constantly between genres and produced work in every form: from poetry and drama through short stories, a novel and critical essays, to the long prison letter *De Profundis*. There is also little sense of development in Wilde's work, possibly because of his movement between genres, but more probably, as I will try to show, because his ideas were substantially formed early on in his career, and he rehearsed and re-expressed them with little variation. In many ways his work is not as radical as has been argued. He can be seen to represent the end of certain strands of nineteenth-century thought, and, even if in others he does have a connection to the future shape of literature and social relations, it is not one that is out of its time, but rather one that is firmly rooted in the late-Victorian period. In the chapters that follow I shall take three periods of Wilde's life – his education at Oxford, the years of his public success, and the events surrounding his trials and imprisonment – to discuss the work and ideas connected with them, and to demonstrate that the symbolic relation to the age in which he declared that he stood was not necessarily always that of subversion or opposition.

1

Making the Self

Oscar Wilde was born in Dublin on 16 October 1854. His mother, Jane, had already adopted the pen name 'Speranza' and was celebrated for her poetry and articles in support of the nascent Irish Nationalist Movement; and his father, William, was a surgeon who was knighted for his work on the Irish Census. Wilde attended school near Dublin, doing well academically and winning a scholarship to Trinity College. He was already talented in Greek and deeply interested in classical Greek literature and culture, and at Trinity he began his enthusiasm for the Aesthetic movement in art and literature. In 1874 he sat for a scholarship to Oxford, which he won, enrolling at Magdalen College in the autumn. At Oxford he found himself in an agreeable environment, one that suited his social aspirations but that also provided him with the intellectual impetus that was to propel him through his life. In this chapter I shall look at Wilde's intellectual development, and discuss the profound impact that his undergraduate studies subsequently had upon him and his work. At Oxford Wilde was exposed to some of the most influential and controversial thinkers of the nineteenth century – the art historians and theorists John Ruskin and Walter Pater; the Professor of Greek Benjamin Jowett; the Professor of Moral Philosophy William Wallace – as well as to the work being done on human history and society in the wake of Charles Darwin's theorization of evolution through natural selection.

The years between the summer of 1878 and his departure for America in 1881 were ones of transition for Wilde. In July 1878, at Oxford, with what he called 'a display of fireworks' (*L.* 70), he took a first in Greats and won the prestigious Newdigate

Prize for Poetry, but he was obliged to remain for another term to re-attempt a failed exam in Divinity in order to be awarded his degree. Despite his success in Finals, he saw little prospect of a Fellowship, and a career in poetry could hardly be sustained on his precarious income. As he had declared to friends, 'Somehow or other I'll be famous, and if not famous notorious' (E. 45), the only possible move was to go to London, and to attempt to enter literary and cultural society. He seems to have spent a period itinerant between Oxford and London, and in a letter of December 1878 he wrote of how busy he was looking for lodgings and making literary friends. Early in 1879 he moved into rooms with his friend Frank Miles in Salisbury Street, and Wilde continued the process of constructing the persona that he had begun at Oxford. While at university he had experimented with various possibilities; he skirted around the Catholic Church, as he was to do all his life until he was finally received into the Church while on his deathbed; he joined the university Masonic Lodge, which he seems to have enjoyed principally for its costume; he made forays into the House Beautiful in furnishing his rooms; he travelled in Greece and Italy, and made an appearance at the opening of the new Grosvenor Gallery that attracted attention because of his fantastical outfit. In London he formed friendships and cultivated acquaintances in all parts of literary, theatrical and society life. In July 1880 he and Miles moved to Tite Street, Chelsea, into a house designed by Godwin, who had been the architect of the controversial painter James Whistler's house. Whistler himself was a neighbour in Tite Street and for some years a rather awkward friend and rival, until there was a decisive breach between them.

During this time Wilde was working hard, writing reviews, poetry and prose, and in 1881 his play *Vera, or the Nihilists* was privately printed and his volume *Poems* published. Both of these proved to be problematic. Wilde circulated Vera among his theatrical friends and acquaintances, including Ellen Terry and Henry Irving, but none showed any interest in producing or performing in it. The play was finally accepted by Mrs Bernard Beere, and performance scheduled for December 1881, but, possibly as a reaction to the assassinations in that year of Tsar Alexander II and President Garfield, it was withdrawn just before rehearsals began. The volume of poems caused controversy in Oxford, where the secretary of the Union had asked Wilde for a copy, which had then been denounced as immoral and derivative, resulting in a vote being taken and the presentation copy refused and returned. Closer to home, Frank Miles's father also objected to the poems, and to one in particular, probably 'Charmides', which, among other fervid moments, describes a young man's sexual encounter with a statue. Wilde was obliged to leave Tite Street and had to stay with his mother for some months before he took new rooms off Grosvenor Square.

But 1881 was not solely a year of disappointment and difficulty. Wilde had been enthusiastic for the new movement of Aestheticism since his time at Trinity College, and had come to know a number of the English writers and artists associated with it. Aestheticism was the avant-garde movement of its time; it espoused a philosophy of art and a philosophy of life and thus became both a literary/artistic and a social phenomenon. In its simplest definition the Aesthetic movement was identified with the idea of 'art for art's sake': that art should not be required to convey moral values and that the experience of art is the highest of all human experience. For the Aesthetes, the aim was to live in the manner of art, to transform everyday life into a work of art in itself. The movement was regarded with suspicion and outright hostility by the mainstream of Victorian thinkers, who were strongly attached to a more utilitarian idea of art as a realist medium for the representation of society and moral values. The Aesthetes were a conspicuous target as their philosophy led them to cultivate extravagant dress and home decoration, and their opinions on beauty were easily parodied.

Whistler and Wilde had already been parodied in plays and by George du Maurier in a sequence of caricatures of the 'fleshly poet' Maudle and the aesthete painter Postlethwaite in *Punch* when Gilbert and Sullivan's opera *Patience* opened in April. The opera was a full musical parody of the movement, and audiences were easily able to understand the objects of the satire. Even though the two aesthetes, Bunthorne and Grosvenor, were composite types, Wilde and Whistler were readily identified. *Patience* had already opened in New York and was doing well when the producer of Gilbert and Sullivan's operas, Richard D'Oyly Carte, who also promoted lecture tours, suggested that Wilde undertake a tour of America, with the idea that the two productions would be mutually profitable. Aestheticism had a far lower profile in the United States and no single figures with whom it could be associated. As Carte wrote to an American booking agent:

> if Mr Wilde were brought to this country with the view of illustrating in a public way his idea of the aesthetic . . . not only would society be glad to hear the man and receive him socially, but also . . . the general public would be interested in hearing from him a true and correct definition and explanation of the latest form of fashionable madness. (E. 145)

It is clear that Wilde was intended to illustrate Aestheticism as much as to lecture on it, and, whereas the *Patience* character Bunthorne was made up as Whistler in Britain, he was acted as Wilde in America. The offer of payment for the tour was a good one, and promised a welcome reprieve from persistent financial difficulties. Wilde put a good deal of preparation into his image for the tour, taking elocution lessons and designing a series of costumes, even if he did leave writing the lecture itself until he actually arrived in New York. Wilde spent the whole of 1882 in the United States and Canada and, despite the rigours of the itinerary, seems to have enjoyed the tour. He delivered three different lectures. The first was 'The English Renaissance of Art', which is reported to have been too long and too theoretical for the audiences, who were expecting entertainment. It was radically adapted to the shorter and more accessible 'The Decorative Arts', the main lecture that he delivered from February onwards. 'The House Beautiful' was the secondary piece for towns where there was more than one engagement.

As well as the showmanship of the lectures, there is a serious core of an intellectual position, particularly in the 'English Renaissance', that is continuous with the developed philosophy of the *Intentions* essays. In this chapter, then, I will look at how Wilde's work emerged; how he made an image for himself as well as developing a critical philosophy of the importance of self-creation. For Wilde, the achievement of an individual identity is crucial, and this idea can be seen in the American lectures and the four essays that were eventually to be collected and published as *Intentions* (1891). In 'The Truth of Masks' first published in 1885, 'Pen, Pencil and Poison' (1889), 'The Decay of Lying' (1889) and 'The Critic as Artist' (1890), the question of the perfection of the self, which appears in a deliberately trivialized form as superficial and external decoration in the presentation of the lectures, is what drives Wilde's writing, as it does in all the genres he explores. Wilde's self-creation is not simple publicity-seeking, nor is it to be accounted for only by reference to his undoubted participation in the burgeoning commodity culture of the late Victorian age. It springs from a principled philosophical position, the fundamental element of which is the continuous process of the refinement and perfection of the individual self. This seems not to have been a position very easily arrived at: at Oxford Wilde experienced frustration at his own contradictions, seeing them as weakness and self-deception, and this untitled poem expresses similar self-criticism:

I shift with every changing creed,
No better than a broken reed
Less stable than the shifting sand
Less stable than the changing sea
At every setting of the sun
I cry in vain, 'What have I done
This day for immortality?'

(*CW* 765)

He came, however, to see contradictions as strengths, and permanence and consistency of thought and character as doctrinaire and dulling of the spirit. It is from acceptance of flux that he also comes to embrace paradox as the symbolic expression and enactment of the creative process. Across all the genres in which he wrote, paradox is the persistent mode of his work, and this chapter will argue that Wilde's use of it represents a great deal more than the mere flourish of rhetorical brilliance, and demonstrate self-contradiction as a reality pervading art, the artist and the world.

Despite the obvious self-creation that is apparent in Wilde's social behaviour and the caricature that the American lecture persona colludes with, Wilde's philosophical position and intellectual basis were solid and serious. Moreover, as I have suggested, there is little development in Wilde's work across his career; he moves between genres, but the foundations of his thought remain unchanged. This is not because, as some earlier critics have implied, his work is thin, or indeed, as he said, that he put his genius into his life instead of his work, but because the principles of his ideas already contain the concepts of change and process within them. His studies at Oxford are of profound importance. Two notebooks survive from that period, a commonplace book of notable extracts such as many Victorians kept, as well as a notebook that seems to be one that was started in preparing the essay 'The Rise of Historical Criticism', which he submitted for the Chancellor's Essay Prize. The range of his reading is clear, but there is also a striking comparison between the notebooks and his requests for books submitted while he was in prison twenty years later. The prison lists request several works on Christianity and a number of books published since his incarceration, but alongside these many of the same texts from the notebooks reappear. In prison he asks for, among others, E. B. Tylor's *Primitive Culture* (not approved by the Governor), W. H. Lecky's *History of the Rise and Influence of the Spirit of Rationalism in Europe* (also not approved), H. T. Buckle's *History of Civilization in England*, Ernst Renan's *Life of Jesus* and Walter Pater's essays, all of which are quoted from and referred to at length in the Oxford notebooks. What is also clear in reading the notebooks is that ideas and whole phrases appear again, unchanged, in the essays that ten years later make up *Intentions*, and even later in the plays and *De Profundis*. Wilde's ideas and beliefs are formed from a particular nexus of Victorian thought, one that centres on Oxford in the latter half of the nineteenth century.

The twin stars of the Oxford art history firmament were John Ruskin and Walter Pater. Ruskin had been appointed Slade Professor of Fine Art in 1870 and he is remembered for his impact on the Pre-Raphaelites and for his championing of Gothic architecture, which changed the face of English churches. Ruskin's attachment to the Gothic was founded in his belief in the continuity of art and life, from which he derived an ideal of the democratic function of the imagination in creating art and culture for the purpose of improvement. He believed in social reform through aesthetic response; that through attention to the moral meanings in nature, true art would be created, and through appreciation of art, humanity could refine its spirit, learn to act unselfishly and break down the boundaries between nature, art and life. 'Art is the work of the whole spirit of man; and as that spirit is, so is the deed of it: and by whatever power of vice or virtue any art is produced, the same vice or virtue it reproduces or teaches.'[1] Ruskin's is an idealist perspective, anti-materialist and anti-utilitarian in both culture and politics, and he was also strongly opposed to the growing movement of Aestheticism. His famous attack on Whistler came from this opposition: he had expressed similar ideas in the 1877 lectures from his work *Modern Painters*, which are deeply critical of materialism, and voice his concerns about art criticism becoming the 'mere operation of sense'. Wilde knew Ruskin's work well and even participated in Ruskin's famous practical application of his theory, the plan to build a road with hedges and wild-flower borders in the Oxfordshire countryside. After several weeks of rising early and wheeling barrows of stones, Wilde and his fellow artisans were released from their labour when Ruskin departed for Venice and the road-building ceased.

Walter Pater took up his fellowship in 1864, and his book *The Renaissance* (originally entitled *Studies in the History of the Renaissance*) was first published in 1873, the year before Wilde went up to Oxford. *The Renaissance* was partly a challenge to Ruskin's work, as Pater's is an argument for aesthetic hedonism based on individual contemplation and enjoyment of sensual experience, without the drive to social engagement that Ruskin's aesthetic produced. Pater's work had a profound effect on an entire generation of undergraduates, an effect that was nervously predicted by some critics on publication, and Pater in fact omitted the most controversial section of the book, the Conclusion, in the second edition (1877), because he 'conceived it might possibly mislead some of those young men into whose hands it might fall'.[2] Wilde acknowledged the effect of *The Renaissance* upon him. In *De Profundis* he calls it 'that book which has had such a strange influence over my life' (*CW*

1022), and many people were keen to identify it as the 'poisonous' book in *The Picture of Dorian Gray*.

Pater's essays in *The Renaissance* are notoriously inaccurate in matters of fact, perhaps deliberately so, as he commented in an article in the *Westminster Review* in 1866: 'To the modern spirit nothing is, or can be rightly known, except relatively and under conditions.' *The Renaissance* is much less a critical study than a series of essays on temperament, a description of a kind of sensibility that is marked by receptivity and responsiveness to perception. Crucial to Pater's aesthetic philosophy are openness to experience and the careful calibration of the effects of experience without allowing any permanent imprint to be retained. Thus he sees the Renaissance not simply as a cultural movement but as a manifestation of a particular spirit, which leads him to find it not just in fifteenth-century Italy, but also in twelfth-century France and eighteenth-century Germany, and always manifested in particular individuals. It is also for Pater a modern philosophy, a response to and a means of managing continuous change. This is the infamous assertion from the Conclusion:

> To burn always with this hard, gem-like flame, to maintain this ecstasy, is success in life. In a sense it might even be said that our failure is to form habits: for, after all, habit is relative to a stereotyped world, and meantime it is only the roughness of the eye that makes any two persons, things, situations, seem alike. While all melts under our feet, we may well grasp at any exquisite passion, or any contribution to knowledge that seems by a lifted horizon to set the spirit free for a moment, or any stirring of the senses, strange dyes, strange colours, and curious odours, or the work of the artist's hands, or the face of one's friend . . . What we have to do is to be for ever curiously testing new opinions and courting new impressions, never acquiescing in a facile orthodoxy, of Comte, or of Hegel, or of our own.[3]

In Pater's aesthetics all orthodoxy is facile, as is any repeated response that threatens to form habits. There is no way to accumulate experience or to develop the self; the true renaissance spirit must be ready anew at each experience, without the traces of former responses. This is in contrast to Ruskin, for whom the purpose of the refinement of the eye was to see into a truth in art or in the world that would lead to a permanent reconstitution of the consciousness, and the awakening of the love for freedom of spirit that is expressed in the best art. Ruskin sees this awakening as leading to a desire for general social liberty, and to the dynamic interchange of the free energy of creativity between art and life. Although the work is for the individual to pursue, it leads to a collective sense. In Pater the self is entirely solipsistic; relations with others are only a source of quickening and multiplying the self.

The title of Wilde's original American lecture, 'The English Renaissance in Art', speaks directly of his debt to Pater, as does his opening definition:

> I call it our English Renaissance because it is indeed a sort of new birth of the spirit of man, like the great Italian Renaissance of the fifteenth century, in its desire for a more gracious and comely way of life, its passion for physical beauty, its exclusive attention to form, its seeking for new subjects for poetry, new forms of art, new intellectual and imaginative enjoyments . . . it is our most recent expression of beauty. (*EL* 112)

He aligns himself with Pater here in his insistence on both the modernity of this position and its continuity with a great tradition that is situated at what Pater called 'the sharp apex of the present moment between two hypothetical eternities'.[4] There is much else that echoes Pater in the American lectures. This, for example, sounds like a version of the 'Conclusion': 'No longer the permanent, the essential truths of life that are treated of; it is the momentary situation of the one, the momentary aspect of the other that art seeks to render' (*EL* 113). There is also a good deal that is very close to Ruskin: 'Art will do more than make our lives joyous and beautiful; it will become part of the new history of the world and a part of the brotherhood of man' (*CW* 934), and even more clearly perhaps here: 'The most practical school of morals in the world, the best educator, is true art; it never lies, never misleads, and never corrupts, for all good art, all high art, is founded on honesty, sincerity and truth' (*CW* 936). This seems to be far from the aphorisms that preface *Dorian Gray*, 'All art is quite useless' or 'No artist has ethical sympathies', but I would suggest that this is not the case, because Wilde had already developed different conceptions of ethics and utility.

Some of the difficulty of the 'English Renaissance' lecture, and perhaps the reason that it was found to be long and overly theoretical, is because Wilde is beginning to articulate publicly a new position for himself, one that will depart from Pater. The divergence from Pater that is already detectable in the lectures comes from the other side of Wilde's Oxford learning. Ruskin and Pater were crucial to Wilde, and their influence has been noted and explored in detail by many critics, but what has received far less attention is the network of other, very different thinkers, who had an equal, if not greater, impact upon his philosophy. There were other powerful influences at Oxford. Among the most important of these were Benjamin Jowett, Professor of Greek, and William Wallace, eventually Professor of Moral Philosophy, but a teaching Fellow during Wilde's undergraduate years. Jowett published *The Dialogues of Plato* in 1875 and Wallace *The Logic of Hegel* in 1874, a translation with Wallace's long essay on Hegel, 'Prolegomena', as its introduction. There are many references and ideas from these two newly published books in Wilde's notebooks, and also prominent are a surprising number of references to contemporary scientific and socio-scientific texts: Herbert Spencer's *The Study of Sociology* (1873), E. B. Tylor's *Primitive Culture* (1871), T. H. Huxley's essays, John Tyndall's *Fragments of Science* (1874) and W. K. Clifford's *Lectures and Essays* (1879), as well as several Social Darwinist-influenced histories of civilization.

Between them, these texts form the second major axis of Wilde's thought and the principal means by which he comes to differ from Pater. Jowett and Wallace were part of a group of English scholars and expositors of Hegel, and they both read his ideas on the unfolding of history in the context of the post-Darwinian notions of change that are also demonstrated in Spencer, Huxley and Tylor. The Oxford Hegelians focused on the notion of the dialectic in Hegel, the three-stage process in thought where the first stage is a primary position of unified affirmation, within which arises a second stage of difference or negation. The testing of these against one another gives rise to a third stage, a new and more complex thought that still preserves within it the contradictory elements. The dialectic is not a series of random changes in thought, but a progressive unfolding of the purpose of history, the movement towards the completed realization of what Hegel called *Geist*, or pure Mind. For Jowett and Wallace, Hegel's dialectical motion of development towards perfection meshed with what had become the dominant received idea of Darwinism: that nature too moved in this fashion. The Oxford Hegelians saw evolution as the common law of physical, mental, social and historical development, with the inheritance of acquired characteristics accounting for the evolving towards perfection, the realization of the Absolute. Perhaps one of the reasons that this aspect of Wilde's thought has been less discussed is that this unified theory is so peculiar to the late Victorian moment; it emerged in opposition to the empiricism of Hume, Locke and Mill, and it has no contemporary legacy or resonance, the empirical tradition in British philosophy having been rapidly reasserted with the logical positivism and ordinary language philosophy of the twentieth century. It is, however, a moment that catches Wilde and defines him in that time and place, against the contemporaneity that is now so frequently claimed for him. The influence of the Hegelians on Wilde was strong; it lasted all his life and can be seen in his work long after he left the immediate environment of Oxford. He understood the implications clearly: one of Wilde's many notes from Wallace reads: 'Hegelian dialectic is the natural selection produced by a struggle for existence in world of thought' (*NB* 149), and his undergraduate essay 'The Rise of Historical Criticism' represents a Hegelian account of the unfolding of a scientific historical method in Greek civilization and culture, very thoroughly founded in these contemporary readings of the relations of historical, methodological, social and individual development .

It is also important to remember Wilde's classical scholarship and particularly his interest and notable ability in Greek. It has been suggested that Jowett's legacy was in some respects a difficult one.[5] He sought to establish a Hellenic ideal in which the systematic study of Greek culture would provide transcendent values as an alternative to Christian theology. His influence on a generation of men of the ruling class of Britain and its empire was great, but his encouragement of the Greek model of intense relationships between men stopped decidedly with the intellectual, refusing the suggestions in the Greek texts of the carnality of male relations. For some of his disciples, like John Addington Symonds (whom I shall discuss further in Chapter 3), there was a painful tension in Jowett's teaching that, on one hand, valorized the Greek culture that appeared to vindicate erotic or sexual love for men, but on the other emphatically denied that love as unnatural. Wilde's poem 'Hélas!' can be read as dramatizing such a conflicted position:

> To drift with every passion till my soul
> Is a stringed lute upon which all winds can play,
> Is it for this that I have given away
> Mine ancient wisdom and austere control?
> Methinks my life is a twice-written scroll
> Scrawled over on some boyish holiday
> With idle songs for pipe and virelay
> Which do but mar the secret of the whole.
> Surely there was a time I might have trod
> The sunlit heights, and from life's dissonance
> Struck one clear chord to reach the ears of God:
> Is that time dead? Lo! With a little rod
> I did but touch the honey of romance –
> And must I lose a soul's inheritance?

(*CW* 864)

The opening lines speak of the Paterian ideal condition of openness to all experience, which is then countered by the Greek inheritance of austere control. He suggests the difficulty of living in the contradictions of his 'twice-written' life and the experience of dissonance in ways that recall his earlier frustrations in attempting to reconcile them into a dialectical achievement. The last lines gesture towards the problem of the erotic, the active experience of beauty rather than its contemplative appreciation. I shall discuss the influence of the representation of Greek sexuality in the third chapter, but, in the context of his philosophical ideas, Jowett's work was still of great importance to Wilde. Jowett saw the dialogic form of Plato's writings as analogous to the Hegelian dialectic; another of Wilde's notes reads: 'The normal conditions of progress in thought is this: first a narrow definiteness, an uncompromising dogmatism *then* the antagonism and criticism to which this gives rise lastly the intellectual synthesis and union: (Hegel)' (*NB* 123).

It is in this embrace of the Hegelian/evolutionary unfolding towards perfection that the departure from the pure Aestheticism of Pater arises, in the question of the ideal constitution of self-consciousness. Pater described his novel *Marius the Epicurean* as a fuller dealing of the issues raised in the Conclusion of *The Renaissance,* and at the close of the novel, when Marius is near to death, he reflects upon his life:

> Surely, the aim of a true philosophy must lie, not in futile efforts towards the complete accommodation of man to the circumstances in which he chances to find himself, but in the maintenance of a kind of candid discontent, in the face of the very highest achievement; the unclouded and receptive soul quitting the world finally, with the same fresh wonder with which it had entered the world still unimpaired, and going on its blind way at last with the consciousness of some profound enigma in things, but as a pledge of something further to come.[6]

In *Marius,* the self is a blank, 'the tablet of the mind white and smooth'; no personality is present in the utterly passive contemplative mind:

> Revelation, vision, the discovery of a vision, the *seeing* of a perfect humanity, in a perfect world . . . he had always set that above the *having,* or even the *doing,* of anything. For, such vision, if received with due attitude on his part, was, in reality, the *being* something.[7] (emphasis in original)

In what could be a deliberate echo of Pater, Wilde writes in 'The Critic as Artist': 'the contemplative life, the life that has for its aim not *doing* but *being,* and not *being* merely, but *becoming* – that is what the critical spirit can give us' (*CW* 1038–9). He paraphrases Pater, and reproduces his italic emphasis, but moves beyond the 'mere' being that Marius embodies to a dynamic becoming. In Wilde the extra step is the Hegelian motion towards the Absolute, a movement towards a completed state, even if that completed state is never to be reached. Where Pater's ideal is a stasis of receptivity, Wilde's contains an implicit accomplishment. In 'The English Renaissance' lecture Wilde states directly: 'the good we get from art is not what we learn from it; it is what we become through it' (*EL* 150); again the anti-utilitarian position emphasizes the *becoming* against the mere *being*. Although Hegel regarded art as the lowest of the three forms through which the dialectic moved, Wilde prioritizes it as the means by which not only the self, but society, can become realized. This is moving quite some way from the 'art for art's sake' that is the shorthand definition of Paterian Aestheticism; Wilde's Oxford education allows him to tie together Plato, Aristotle, Hegel, Darwin and Spencer in the belief that human, social and biological organisms are guided in their development by internal plans. Existence can be more than simply being; instead it can be a development, the realization of an individual potential that is also inherent in the material universe.

In the final lines of 'The Truth of Masks' Wilde explicitly expresses and links his influences in what could be seen as a brief statement of his manifesto. The statement appears rather abruptly; the rest of the essay is a long discursion on the necessity of historical accuracy of costume in productions of Shakespeare, but it ends with what seems to be an entirely unrelated short section in which Wilde says that he disagrees with much that he has written, and that it simply represents an 'artistic standpoint':

> For in art there is no such thing as a universal truth. A Truth in art is that whose contradictory is also true. And just as it is only in art-criticism, and through it, that we can apprehend the Platonic theory of ideas, so it is only in art-criticism, and through it, that we can realize Hegel's system of contraries. The truths of metaphysics are the truths of masks. (*CW* 1173)

Masks are multiple personalities: as Pater advocates the 'quickened, multiplied consciousness', so does Wilde, but his multiple personality is continually changing, because it can then act as the crucible for the experience of dialectical development. If we read these assertions in the light of a Hegelian framework, then they carry a meaning very different from the ideas of concealment, secrecy and the double life that are usually read into them. Although the collection of essays appeared as *Intentions* in 1891, all the individual pieces had been previously published: 'The Decay of Lying', 'The Critic as

Artist' and 'The Truth of Masks' in *The Nineteenth Century* and 'Pen, Pencil and Poison' in the *Fortnightly Review* (which under the editorship of Frank Harris had provided something of a forum for the discussion of radical Darwinism), and they had been read without too much alarm, and certainly without the real or pretended outrage that they engendered during and after the trials. The ideas seemed less new to his contemporaries than has perhaps been imagined, because the later readings participate in the post-scandal desire to see the evidence of sexual unorthodoxy in what was not necessarily a critically radical position. These essays, along with 'The Soul of Man under Socialism', are the core and the most expanded expression of Wilde's critical and artistic position, and I will now look at some of the ideas they represent around the issues of the relations of life to art, the role of the critic, morality and progress.

In 'The Decay of Lying' Wilde utilizes the masks of Cyril and Vivian to discuss the proper form of art, which, as Vivian proposes, is the lie. The deliberately provocative recommendation of lying, however, is really only the valuing of creative invention over imitation. The effect of the essay is achieved by the substitution of the word 'lying' where the word 'imagination' would be. Lying is straightforwardly equated with true art, in that both show complete disregard for facts. Lying is not falsification – Wilde ascribes that to politicians – but anti-realism, standing against the dominance of quotidian experience. In fact the quotidian is hardly recognized as experience at all. It is characterized simply as repetition or as imitation of actions, and realism in fiction or painting as a mutual reinforcement of stagnation. In 'Critic' Gilbert identifies the source of the failure of life as 'the thing that lends to life its sordid security, the fact that one can never repeat exactly the same emotion' (*CW* 1132), whereas art does allow the repetition of emotion. This is not a contradiction of the rejection of realism as repetition, but the statement that the emotions of art are separated from life and are part of a permanent realm that can remove the reader or viewer from the unproductive, because unrealized, repetition of existence. The same idea is presented in 'The English Renaissance' lecture:

> The simple utterance of joy is not poetry any more than a mere personal cry of pain, and the real experiences of the artist are always those which do not find their direct expression but are gathered up and absorbed into some artistic form which seems, from such real experiences, to be the farthest removed and the most alien. (*EL* 127)

Realism for Wilde is an imitative action; it provides nothing new, whereas true art should provide new ideals that lead to development. This again can be seen as an example of Wilde's Hegelianism, in which lying is conceptualized as that which is non-identical to the everyday form and stimulates the dialectic motion that pushes forwards towards the realization of perfection inherent in existence. In the refiguring of realism as the genuinely decadent form it is also a sly rebuttal of the characterization of his position as decadent. Vivian argues that art began as purely imaginative abstract decoration, then 'takes life as part of her rough material' and re-creates it, remaining still indifferent to fact. But the third stage is the triumph of realism, when art is sacrificed to representation. 'This', he says, 'is the true decadence, and it is from this that we are now suffering' (*CW* 1078). The only bad art comes from the return to Nature, but these prescriptions are not quite as easy as they sound. Vivian recounts the tragic tale of a woman who lived out the life of the heroine of a story because she, and others, believed herself to resemble the initial description of the heroine. Vivian has produced this anecdote as proof of the fact that life imitates art more often than art imitates life, but the real message of the tale is that even art should not be imitated in a slavishly uncritical fashion. Art is not the plot for a life, but the creation of an image of the truth of experience that can then stimulate further acts of creation, not imitation. Vivian's summary definition of lying as 'the telling of beautiful untrue things' (*CW* 1091) is an apparently paradoxical inversion of Keats's line 'Beauty is truth, truth beauty', but the sense is actually the same: what the world regards as untrue is simply unfactual, and for Wilde the unfactual, the imaginative, is the truth.

Crucial in Wilde's conceptualization of art is not only the creative faculty, but the critical too. In the essays in *Intentions* he redefines the role of the critic by expanding it so widely that it is hardly differentiated from that of the artist. 'The Critic as Artist' is another Platonic dialogue between two characters, Ernest and Gilbert, and it could equally well be entitled 'The Artist as Critic' as it collapses those two roles into the enactment of a single spirit. This is much as Pater does in *The Renaissance*, where artists and critics are treated as equal manifestations of the Renaissance consciousness, but, as in almost every example in Wilde's philosophy, his Paterian ideas are inflected with the version of Hegel that he learned from Jowett and Wallace. Wilde says in the essay: 'Creation is always behind the age. It is Criticism that leads us. The Critical Spirit and the World Spirit are one' (*CW* 1154). 'Spirit' is the usual translation of Hegel's *Geist*, the progressive realization of perfection. For Wilde, the spirit of the age is most fully realized in the awakened consciousness of the critic/artist. This consciousness is self-consciousness, and thus to be found in the individual, the personality. The achievement that Wilde seeks for himself and advocates for others is the accomplishment of individuality in the personality; as he puts it elsewhere in the essay, 'as art springs from personality, so it is only to personality that it can be revealed, and from the meeting of the two comes right interpretative criticism' (*CW* 1131). There is no ego-less blank tablet in Wilde's formation; the experiences to which the self must be constantly open, and indeed actively seeking, are formative. Individualism for Wilde is not about the construction of the single stable self, and perfection is not the gaining of a core of identity that is then a solid platform from which to view and to understand the world. He takes his proof from Hegel, and again the source is William Wallace's 'Prolegomena' to *The Logic of Hegel*: 'To the idealistic and speculative reason the object and the subject, the Ego and the Non-Ego are really one. The mind does not come forth equipped to conquer the world, nor is the world a prey prepared for a spoiler – they are both the result of a process' (*NB* 127). This suggests the dissolution of the boundary between subject and object, between critic and art, or perhaps more accurately the perception that the boundaries are real but in constant dynamic tension in a process where the acts of creation and interpretation are the same. The individual must perceive and participate in that process and thus must accept, and indeed celebrate, flux, contradiction and multiplicity as the manifestations of the process.

The rejection of realism is a logical corollary of this position. Wilde goes against Ruskin's insistence on the expressive nature of art to assert that it is the opposite: art and criticism are pure impression. Art is produced from the impression made by experience of life, and does not express life but reproduces impression. Likewise, criticism does not attempt to explain the art object but to manifest the impression of it that, ideally, will be the match and understanding of the original artistic impulse, 'occupying the same relation to creative work that creative work does to the world of form and colour, or the unseen world of passion and thought' (*CW* 1130). The pursuit of personality is the only responsibility of life and art.

Inevitably, this position was seen by some commentators both as frivolous and, in a more sinister light, as advocating immorality. The essays provocatively invite this, as they do with their praise of lying, but they invite the perception of immorality deliberately in order that readers must question what a real definition of morality might be and therefore have a real intellectual understanding of any idea they choose to hold. Gilbert, in 'Critic', states this directly, saying that most people have so little understanding of what thought is that 'they seem to imagine that, when they have said that a theory is dangerous, they have pronounced its condemnation, whereas it is only such theories that have any true intellectual value. An idea that is not dangerous is unworthy of being called an idea at all' (*CW* 1141). Wilde's constant drawing of attention to the question of immorality is the sign that he does not consider his ideas or his works to be immoral at all.

Wilde's moral scheme is not a retrospective position constructed in defence at the trials; it is very fully present in *Intentions*, and encapsulated in the infamous aphorism that prefaces *The Picture of Dorian Gray*: 'There is no such thing as a moral or an immoral book. Books are well-written, or badly written. That is all' (*CW* 17). The argument lies in the distinction between ethics and aesthetics, and Wilde's insistence that the two spheres are absolutely distinct and separate. Ethics belongs to the sphere of actions, and aesthetics to that of thought.

> [Modern journalism] serve[s] to show how extremely limited is the area over which ethics, and ethical considerations, can claim to exercise influence. Science is out of the reach of morals, for her eyes are fixed upon eternal truths. Art is out of the reach of morals, for her eyes are fixed upon things beautiful and immortal and ever-changing. (*CW* 1145)

Wilde does not deny the existence of ethical considerations, but seeks to reverse what he sees as the tendency of contemporary society to collapse social and 'moral' prejudices with ethics, and to assume the relevance of this unexamined reflex response to all aspects of existence. He suggests that ethics have taken the place of thought in society: 'Any preoccupation with ideas of right and wrong in conduct shows an arrested intellectual development' (*CW* 1245). If we return to the statement in 'The Critic as Artist' about the relation of ethics and aesthetics, there is also another sense in which this can be understood: as exemplifying the moral neutrality of evolution.

> By revealing to us the absolute mechanism of all action, and so freeing us from the self-imposed and trammelling burden of moral responsibility, the scientific principle of Heredity has become, as it were, the warrant for the contemplative life. It has shown us that we are never less free than when we try to act. (*CW* 1137)

Wilde marshals the post-Darwinian idea of heredity to suggest that physical existence, and therefore actions, previously conceived of as being performed out of absolute free will, are in fact governed by strict and invisible laws of predetermination. Elsewhere he calls action a 'blind thing dependent on external influences, and moved by an impulse of whose nature it is unconscious' (*CW* 1121). Although thought is itself part of an evolutionary scheme that is subject to conscious determination, it is where true freedom can be found and in which progress can be willed.

'Pen, Pencil and Poison' deals with this question. It is an aesthetic examination of sin, and can be read as a kind of sketch for *The Picture of Dorian Gray* in that it rehearses some of the problematic aspects of the theoretical positions that Wilde holds. In the Oxford notebook he writes: '*Progress* Progress in thought is the assertion of individualism against authority, and progress in matter is the differentiation and specialization of function; those organisms which are entirely subject to external influences do not progress any more than a mind entirely subject to authority' (*NB* 121). In 'The Critic as Artist' he goes further than identifying the simple refusal of authority, moving to discuss deliberately transgressive actions. Sin, in Wilde's Darwinian/Hegelian synthesis, is 'an essential element of progress . . . through its intensified assertion of individualism [sin] saves us from monotony of type. In its rejection of current notions of morality, it is one with the higher ethics' (*CW* 1121). There is an additional distinction in 'Pen, Pencil and Poison' between sin and crime. The forger and poisoner Wainewright is a case study, an audacious addition to Pater's gallery of biographies in *The Renaissance* and a consideration of that artistic/critical spirit manifested in more recent history.

Wainewright figures as man out of time, too early for the present age and therefore prone to some of the vagaries of fashion, and too late for the Italian Renaissance, which would mean that his story could take its place among the other 'charming studies of great criminals'. Nevertheless Wilde is identifying him in that lineage because he is a true artist. 'One can fancy an intense personality being created out of sin,' Wilde says, but there is a confusion of sin and crime, in which crime appears only to be the breaking of the law and sin is the more valuable action that is likely to produce progress. Wilde is at pains to suggest that the material profit from Wainewright's poisonings is small, and that the poisonings were part of the intense personality, having artistic quality in their employment of detail such as the antique rings used to hide the poison. He also identifies in Wainewright those essential elements of the dialectical self. The journalistic pseudonyms and the forgeries are seen as multiplications of personality, and his dandyism as a similar mark of seeking to *be* somebody, rather than to *do* something. This too is his downfall; he is caught 'because of his artistic interest in modern life': he looks out of the window when he should be in hiding. In perhaps the most significant phrase in the essay, the multiplicity of Wainewright's identity is crudely reduced: 'The permanence of personality is a very subtle metaphysical problem, and certainly the English law solves the question in an extremely rough-and-ready manner' (*CW* 1104). Wilde asserts that the worst of Wainewright's sins was his influence on journalistic prose and not his poisonings. The problem in locating sin in the social and legal context is that for Wilde sin is a single action that is necessarily dialectical, and may not be repeated. It is produced in the flux of the changing individual and should not be confused with crime. Crime is the action of a permanent and fixed type of personality, the criminal, and therefore to be punished accordingly. The rough-and-readiness of the law insists that personality types are fixed and cannot recognize multiplicity, a view that was to have terrible consequences for Wilde himself.

Although Wilde refuses the nexus of ethics and morality that he sees in contemporary society, he is left with a problem about the rightness of participation in actions. He has defended the contemplative life, but perceives a difficulty in the modern condition, which is that 'we who are born at the close of this wonderful age are at once too cultured and too critical, too intellectually subtle and too curious of exquisite pleasures, to accept any speculation about life in exchange for life itself' (*CW* 1136). It is as though the very nature of the progress already achieved through contemplation now demands actions. On the one hand, the modern critic/artist is drawn by the world and its fantastic array of sensations and impressions, and, on the other, he is dedicated to the eternal and unworldly ideal. The theoretical problems of what participation in the flux of modernity means, and the effect that this will have on the realization of the individual self, are dramatized first in *The Picture of Dorian Gray* as tragedy and then in the society plays as comedy. Again it is interesting to contrast Wilde's with Pater's position. In the fictional treatments of their philosophies, Wilde's *Dorian Gray* and Pater's *Marius the Epicurean*, there are rather different resolutions, or, if not resolutions, outcomes, to this tension. In *Marius*, the eponymous protagonist is left apparently in the state that Pater warns about in the closing section of the 'Conclusion'. He has not sustained great passion, but is a participant in the outward form of Christianity without his inward assent. Possibly this is Pater's irony, that Marius is treated as a Christian martyr, when in fact he is a martyr to another creed, that of the non-adopting of creeds.

He has become fixed in a posture that begins as open acceptance of all sensation and ends as paralysis in the face of those sensations. In this Marius most closely resembles Lord Henry Wotton, who, at the end of *Dorian Gray*, is in much the same place. By contrast, Dorian's martyrdom can be seen to stand against the resistance to commitment of Pater: 'The theory or idea or system which requires of us the sacrifice of any part of this experience, in consideration of some interest into which we cannot enter, or some abstract theory we have not identified with ourselves, or of what is only conventional, has no real claim upon us.[8] *The Picture of Dorian Gray* can be seen as an opposition between Wilde's idealist, Hegelian, aesthetic humanism as represented in Basil, and Pater's materialist, aesthetic hedonism as represented in Lord Henry, but it is not quite as simple as that, because of the presence of Dorian and the portrait. Dorian has participated in existence but in the manner that Ruskin had feared in Aestheticism. It is the mere indulgence of sense, it is without any realization or productive difference, and it therefore falls further from the ideal. Dorian is one of the figures of perversity that Wilde recognizes as the hidden danger of paradox, where the multiplication of the self can become a pathological growth rather than the sane advancement of life and art. It is significant in Wilde's work that it is a work of art that proves dangerous. In *Dorian Gray* it grows ugly and disgusting, and ultimately causes death, as it also does in 'The Portrait of Mr W. H.'. This is not because the works of art are representative of immoral actions, but because they have failed to contribute to progress. In 'The Critic as Artist' Gilbert demands that conscience be merged in instinct (*CW* 1122), and Dorian's actions lack the self-consciousness that would allow them to be part of the ideal becoming.

When Wilde speaks of 'attaining perfection', it is not the attainment of the kind of negative perfection that Pater envisages, which is a disengagement from life, but an expansion of a Darwinist notion, where perfection is the achievement of individuation in each person and the progress in culture that results from it. It is a clear countering of Pater's refusal in the 'Conclusion' to accept, as he says, that the aim of life is the accommodation of man to the circumstances in which he finds himself. Pater's statement there is a paraphrase of the description of adaptation to environment that is the motor of natural selection, and he explicitly refutes the notion of evolution in the human spirit or society. Wilde, of course, also refuses the crude sense of adaptation to the environment that would entail conformity to the present in terms of superficial, social existence; everything he writes on style from house decoration to dress stands against that. His description of the *becoming* that is the highest aim of aesthetic experience, however, can be read as something like the evolution of the self and society through art. In the last paragraphs of 'Critic' he names Darwin as one of the two reasons that the nineteenth century is the turning point in history, because Darwin is the critic of the book of Nature. The other reason is Renan (who appears in both the Oxford notebooks and the prison reading lists), because he was the critic of the Books of God. In 'Critic' Wilde goes further and suggests that the relation between ethics and aesthetics is the difference between natural selection and sexual selection; that ethics, like natural selection, makes existence possible, and aesthetics, like sexual selection, makes it 'lovely and wonderful', fills it with 'new forms' and gives it 'progress, variety and change' (*CW* 1154). The aim of natural selection is existence, but it is also individuation and complexity, the physiological equivalents of Wilde's achievement of personality.

As first formulated by Darwin, natural selection is not a moral process. In the first edition of *The Origin of Species* Darwin describes it as 'the struggle for existence' and insists that this also includes dependence of one being on another.[9] It is only in later editions that he acknowledges Herbert Spencer's coinage of the phrase 'the survival of the fittest'. It is Spencer's phrase that has come to be more closely identified with evolution, and his term introduces an idea of judgement against a standard of 'fitness' that rapidly becomes part of the translations of natural selection from the natural world to the social. The apparent indifference of nature had long troubled the Victorians. It is expressed in Tennyson's famous (and pre-Darwinian) description of nature in *In Memoriam* as careless of the fate of species, as being 'red in tooth and claw'. The synthesis of Hegel and Darwin was one attempt to give meaning to evolution and to regard it as working to a positive scheme, but this kind of optimistic reading was largely eclipsed by the ideas found in the works of thinkers like Huxley and Spencer, where evolutionary success or failure is seen as morally coded.

There is an irony, as so frequently seems to be true in discussing Wilde, in his enthusiastic embrace of the evolutionary metaphor, because, against his sometimes euphorically optimistic reading of them, there is a much darker thread in many of the post-Darwinist works in which the dynamic forward motion becomes far less assured and progress more precarious. In Spencer and Huxley particularly, but also in Tylor and to some extent the other scientific writers Wilde read, there is a preoccupation with what was imagined as the backward movement of evolution. This had been articulated by the biologist Edwin Ray Lankester, who wrote: 'we are accustomed to regard ourselves as necessarily progressing, as necessarily having arrived at a higher and more elaborated condition . . . and as destined to progress still further . . . it is well to remember that we are subject to the general laws of evolution, and are as likely to degnerate as to progress.'[10] Almost from the moment of the publication of *Origin of Species* the empirical observation of living organisms and their comparison with the fossil record had suggested that some organisms actually simplified over time, rather than becoming ever more sophisticated and complex in their organizational structure. As with the application of the theory of natural selection to humans, in the application of this 'de-evolution' it was not long before it was being used to understand human society and especially to frame particular concerns about the present. Lankester, Huxley and Spencer are only a few among many voices expressing the anxieties for social and moral human structures prompted by the implications of the simplification of organisms. By the 1890s the notion of what had come to be called degeneration is strongly, albeit very diversely, developed, with frequent and explicit expression of the connection between de-evolved physiology, moral decline and degenerate cultural production in a wide range of fictional and non-fictional texts.

The irony in Wilde's case is that he believes very strongly in evolution having meaning, and of there being value in those elements of culture and thought that are selected, but equally he is himself cast and frequently cited as a major example of the degenerate type. Max Nordau's highly popular and influential book *Degeneration*, which came out in English in the year of Wilde's imprisonment, discusses Wilde directly in the chapter on 'ego-mania' and describes the Decadents and Aesthetes (of which he calls Wilde the chief) as the 'refuse of civilized peoples'.[11] Wilde believed himself to be at the forefront of the evolutionary type, part of a Renaissance, yet he was persistently characterized as the absolute opposite, the representative of degeneration. This is really the heart of the struggle around questions of morality and Wilde's work. It is seen most starkly in the courtroom of the trials, where Wilde is attempting, and failing, to assert the positive and progressive nature of his philosophy, and his critics and opponents are succeeding in showing that it is evidence of a dangerously regressive motion, and that he is himself the illustration of degeneration.

One of the most interesting points articulated in 'Decay' is the problem that I have already suggested lies deeply, and perhaps fatally, in the tension between novelty and permanence in Wilde's inheritance of Pater's philosophy. The essay explicitly rejects modernity of form and modernity of subject matter as wrong. Modernity of form, it seems, risks the formation of habit. Cyril suggests that a formally modern novel can be amusing only once; that rereading it fails to live up to the true test of art, which is that it can be re-experienced differently. The criticism here is an anticipation of the later argument concerning the death of the avant-garde, that the shock of the new can be experienced only once. It also echoes the manifestos of early Modernism in architecture, with their distinction between novelty and the genuinely new, in which novelty is aligned with the low culture of fashion that requires constant change without advancement, and the truly new is the experience of perceptual adjustment that can be reinvoked at each manifestation and leads to a dialectical change in thought. The rejection of novelty in 'The Decay of Lying' could equally be seen, however, as more akin to Matthew Arnold's definition of culture as 'the best that has been thought and said' and his assertion that true manifestations of culture have a permanence that rises above mere surprise value. There is a very obvious link here too with the conservative Modernism of T. S. Eliot, in which tradition is constantly modified in relation to the genuinely new additions to it. Wilde suggests that properly new art has a relation to a tradition of this kind, and that art that only endeavours to fit with its surroundings is just a product of fashion: 'the more imitative an art is the less it represents to us the spirit of its age' (*CW* 1087), where the spirit of the age is part of the continually unfolding *Geist*, and therefore related to history as a greater whole. The idea of a kind of evolution through aesthetic selection continues in 'The Critic as Artist':

> It seems to me that with the development of the critical spirit we shall be able to realize, not merely our own lives, but the collective life of the race, and so to make ourselves absolutely modern, in the true meaning of the word modernity. For he to whom the present is the only thing that is present, knows nothing of the age in which he lives. To realize the nineteenth century, one must realize every century that has preceded it and contributed to its making. (*CW* 1137)

Here the Darwinian/Hegelian synthesis is again obvious. Development takes place at the level of both individuation and species being. Yet another late-Victorian idea is introduced, and it is one that appears throughout *Intentions*, but particularly in 'Critic': that of 'the race'. Wilde makes very specific reference to the connection between culture and race: 'Do you think it is the imagination that enables us to live these countless lives? Yes; it is the imagination; and the imagination is the result of heredity. It is simply concentrated race-experience' (*CW* 1138). In Intentions it is fidelity to race experience that promises Renaissance, against the true decadence that is the loss of culture. The same passage in 'Critic' quotes Arnold's definition of culture and it is clear that culture, is the manifestation and repository of this distillation of racial identity. Throughout *Culture and Anarchy* Arnold refers to the English race and the necessity of the maintenance and fostering of the culture of that race. This too is Eliot's view, but for Eliot there is far less optimism about the rebirth of culture, the promise of the unfolding of the critical spirit has been lost, and culture is always on the edge of crisis, in decline. Eliot's prescription is an action of recovery, of something like the views that Wilde holds.

It would seem that Wilde comes very close to voicing what is actually a conservative set of ideas, drawn from the complex knot of interpretations and counter-interpretations of the cultural and philosophical positions of the *fin de siècle*. The apparent radicalism of his thought and his embrace of modernity is in fact deeply rooted in the Oxford experience of the 1870s, where the recovery of the true critical/artistic spirit that runs through Europe from classical Greece is the only possible way in which the future can be rescued. If this part of Wilde's philosophy can be seen as congruent with very particular Victorian concerns, I want to turn now to his involvement with some other elements of contemporary culture; to explore his ideas on national identity, socialism and the place of women, and to suggest that these are also deeply marked by late-nineteenth-century experience.

2

Self and Society

In the 1880s Wilde became increasingly successful. Though never comfortably wealthy, he was earning money from his work and he was a fixture in London's social and literary world. He married Constance Lloyd in 1884 and they and their house in Tite Street became examples of fashionable Aesthetic style. Constance gave birth to two sons, Cyril in 1885 and Vyvyan in 1886, and Wilde delighted in their company as they grew older, inventing for them many of the stories that he later published. In the year of Vyvyan's birth Wilde met Robert Ross, who, it has been claimed, was the first of his male lovers.[1] Whatever the truth of that claim, Ross was to be the most loyal of all his friends and the one who devoted himself to securing Wilde's literary legacy. Perhaps more important, and certainly more catastrophic, was Wilde's meeting with Lord Alfred Douglas. They met in 1891, and quickly became involved in the intense relationship that led to the bitter legal battle with Douglas's father, the Marquess of Queensberry, and Wilde's subsequent imprisonment and public disgrace. Wilde's life has inevitably been seen as a series of paradoxes; he was a married homosexual, an Irishman living at the centre of English society and a figure of the social establishment who apparently attacked its cherished values of status, marriage and morality. He has been described as a 'conformist rebel',[2] and in this chapter I will look at the elements of his social criticism in his ideas on socialism and class relations, Irishness, marriage and the place of women. These, and his sexuality, are the main areas in which many contemporary writers have claimed him as modern.

'The Soul of Man under Socialism' was first published in the *Fortnightly Review* in February 1891. Although *Intentions* was published that year, the essay was not included. It seems that Wilde regretted this decision, as when the French translation of the collection was being prepared he wanted to substitute 'The Soul of Man' for 'The Truth of Masks'. This would have made a more coherent volume, as 'Masks' is really an intervention in a limited contemporary debate about costume in Shakespearian drama. Apart from the last few lines, 'Masks' adds nothing to the philosophical positions in the other essays, whereas 'The Soul of Man' continues those positions, even sharing some paragraphs with 'The Critic as Artist'. George Bernard Shaw says in his recollection of Wilde that Robert Ross told him that 'The Soul of Man' had been written after Wilde had heard Shaw give a public lecture on socialism at some time in the late 1880s.[3] Shaw also said that it was very good, even if it had nothing whatever to do with socialism. Shaw's own socialism was of the kind more typical in the late nineteenth century: he was a member of the Fabian Society, which advocated social change through the reform of existing institutions, standing against the revolutionary tenets of more orthodox Marxism.

Wilde's socialism, as it is expressed in 'The Soul of Man', owes more to an extension of aesthetic sensibility. He was influenced in this rather earlier than his apparent inspiration by Shaw: he had long been an admirer of William Morris, whose belief in the potential of art for social change was, in turn, partially owed to Ruskin. Morris's ideas rested on a profound anti-industrialism, and, although he subscribed to Marx and Engels's analysis of the dehumanizing effects produced by the alienation of labour, his solution was far from accepting industrial means of production as the means by which the proletariat might ultimately be freed. For Morris the ideal was a return to a pre-industrial artisan society in which people would find equality and liberty through the expression of their spirit in their work, and the beauty of the environment thus created would ensure continued harmony of existence. At Oxford, Wilde was involved in one of the most well-known practical applications of this idea: Ruskin's road-building project.

A political consciousness is to be found in some of the poetry written before 'The Soul of Man'. There is a little group of sonnets bemoaning the loss of 'Milton's spirit' in England where 'Luxury / With barren merchandise piles up the gate / Where noble thoughts and deeds should enter by' and the land is held by 'ignorant demagogues' (*CW* 774). The Puritan poet seems a curious figure for Wilde's admiration, but in these sonnets Milton stands for a radical republican democracy, the rejection of the mindless accumulation of material goods and a politically committed poetic practice that encourages deep self-reflection. In the longer poem 'Humanitad' Milton is again summoned to witness the moral, spiritual and artistic desecration of England. In this poem there is an explicit link between beauty and social harmony that echoes Morris's pre-industrial fantasy, and more than a faint recollection of that other romantic revolutionary, William Blake: 'the gentle feet / Of Beauty tread no more the stones of each unlovely street . . . Time's worst decay / Will wreathe its ruins with some loveliness, / But these new Vandals can but make a rainproof barrenness' (*CW* 823). Wilde also suggests that 'life is bigger after all / Than any painted angel' and that 'gentle brotherhood, the harmony / Of living in the healthful air, the swift / Clean beauty of strong limbs when men are free' is more wonderful than even the works of Michelangelo or Titian (*CW* 824). There is a lack of clarity about what this brotherhood or freedom actually means, and frequently the sense of social justice seems confused with a much more general sense of liberty, itself confused with a romantic republicanism. Byron is praised for his dedication to the cause of Greek liberation in 'Ravenna', the poem that won Wilde the Newdigate Prize in his final year at Oxford, and he is cited elsewhere as representative, like Milton, of the true poet, one who is constantly engaged in the battle to free the human spirit from the yoke of tyranny.

In 'Ave Imperiatrix' Wilde directly engages with contemporary world politics and speculates that the imperial wars waged by England are the prelude to the rising of 'the young Republic'; that somehow the Empire is an inevitable stage in the progress towards republican freedom. Wilde's nationality is an interesting point in all the poems that are mentioned here: he consistently refers to England, and calls it 'ours', yet, as I shall discuss below, elsewhere he frequently claims an Irish, or at least a Celtic, identity, and his professed republicanism takes on a rather different cast when regarded in the light of

Ireland's colonial struggles during Wilde's lifetime. His republicanism lacks consistency in another respect too, one that is voiced in his sonnet to his friend the actress Ellen Terry in character as Queen Henrietta Maria, where he says that in admiration of her he forgets 'My freedom, and my life republican!' (*CW* 853). Although ostensibly a republican, Wilde admired Queen Victoria, and only a month after his release from prison in 1897 he celebrated her Diamond Jubilee with a party for the children of Berneval, the French village where he was living. Richard Ellmann suggests that his imprisonment had heavily tempered Wilde's radicalism and points out that he enthusiastically supported England during the Boer War, which broke out two years later. This seems very different from his delineation of the costs of imperialism and the espousal of liberty in the poetry, but it must be pointed out that Wilde's radicalism was always of a more cautious, or inconsistent nature. He declared: 'I think I am rather more than a Socialist. I am something of an Anarchist, I believe, but of course, the dynamite policy is very absurd indeed' (E. 273). Yet he was also able to suggest that he would prefer absolutism to anarchy: 'Better the rule of One, whom all obey / Than to let clamorous demagogues betray / Our freedom with the kiss of anarchy' (*CW* 858). In one of his best-known poems, 'Sonnet to Liberty', he expresses his ambivalence, but also reveals the emotional foundation of his political views:

> Not that I love thy children, whose dull eyes
> See nothing save their own unlovely woe,
> Whose minds know nothing, nothing care to know,
> But that the roar of thy Democracies,
> Thy reigns of Terror, thy great Anarchies,
> Mirror my wildest passions like the sea
> And give my rage a brother –! Liberty!
> For this sake only do thy dissonant cries
> Delight my discreet soul, else might all kings
> By bloody knout or treacherous cannonades
> Rob nations of their rights inviolate
> And I remain unmoved – and yet, and yet,
> These Christs that die upon the barricades,
> God knows it I am with them, in some things.
>
> (*CW* 859)

While in America Wilde claimed that this poem no longer represented his political creed, and directed the reporter instead to 'Libertatis Sacra Fames' as an outline of his beliefs.[4] Both display a distrust of anarchy and its violent manifestations, but in the first sonnet there is the suggestion that, while it may not be his political creed, it is perhaps his emotional one. In the first lines he does not sympathize with the revolutionaries, because they lack aesthetic and intellectual aspiration: they are dull and unlovely. His attraction to democracy or anarchy is based in finding a personal and emotional echo of passion and rage in the revolutionary process. He has no attachment to specific causes, only to the *spirit* of revolution, which he feels as a projection of the passion hidden within his otherwise 'discreet' self. However, in the final lines he draws the parallel that he employs so often in his poetry and critical writings: between Christ and the revolutionary.

In 'The Soul of Man under Socialism' Wilde develops the parallel, although the emphasis is modified to describe more accurately Christ's revolutionary character. Wilde insists that Christ's life and teachings do not represent a programme for social change, but one for the perfection of the self. 'Christ made no attempt to reconstruct society, and consequently the Individualism he preached to man could be realized only through pain or in solitude. The Ideals that we owe to Christ are the ideals of the man who abandons society entirely, or of the man who resists society absolutely. But man is naturally social' (*CW* 1196). Wilde's Darwinism again becomes evident in the caveat on humanity's social existence. As I suggested in the previous chapter, unlike many of his contemporaries, Wilde chose to emphasize the description of cooperation within and between organisms that appeared in *The Origin of Species*, and to underplay the more popular general notion that Darwin's theory was a justification of the survival of the fittest. Wilde says in 'The Soul of Man' that 'Evolution is the law of life, and there is no evolution except towards individualism' (*CW* 1194), but his notion of individualism is not the raw competition seen by Spencer and Huxley. It is the perfection of the self that leads to the highest sympathy with others. Wilde also sees Christ's message of self-realization through suffering as a necessary evolutionary stage that it is now possible, in modern society, to surmount. He sees the evolution of society as yet unequally accomplished in the world and suggests that for countries like Russia self-perfection is still possible only through pain, but in others, such as England, the achievement of true individualism is within reach.

> When man has realized Individualism, he will also realize sympathy and exercise it freely and spontaneously. Up to the present man has hardly cultivated sympathy at all. He has merely sympathy with pain, and sympathy with pain is not the highest form of sympathy ... it is tainted with egotism. One should sympathize with the entirety of life, and not with life's sores and maladies merely, but with life's joy and beauty and energy and health and freedom ... Anybody can sympathize with the sufferings of a friend, but it requires a very fine nature – it requires, in fact, that nature of a true Individualist – to sympathize with a friend's success. (*CW* 1195)

What makes modern England ready for the next evolutionary stage is the presence of science and socialism, both of which will eradicate the conditions of pain that encourage the limited type of sympathy:

> while sympathy with joy intensifies the sum of joy in the world, sympathy with pain does not really diminish the amount of pain ... sympathy with consumption does not cure consumption; that is what science does. And when Socialism has solved the problem of poverty, and Science solved the problem of disease, the area of the sentimentalists will be lessened, and the sympathy of man will be large, healthy and spontaneous. (*CW* 1195)

Unsurprisingly, the principal means by which true sympathy and individualism are to be achieved is art. Wilde recognizes that there are certain social conditions that preclude the beautification of life for all people and that the extension of the possibilities of individualism to all will depend upon changes being espoused by those for whom art has already expanded their individual capacities. But it is crucial that this takes the form not of charity, but of agitation. 'Agitators are a set of interfering meddling people, who come down to some perfectly contented class of the community and sow the seeds of discontent amongst them. That is the reason why agitators are so absolutely necessary. Without them, in our incomplete state, there would be no advance towards civilization' (*CW* 1176). Agitators are the evangelists of the message of freedom to those whose horizons have been so narrowed by the ideology of capital that they cannot perceive their own oppression. Unlike the collectivism and greater state control to which Fabian socialism aspired, Wilde's vision of a socialist utopia is one in which people, freed from restraints, have abandoned competition and developed into a community of independent, yet interdependent, individuals. He distinguishes between the false individualism of capitalism and the true individualism of art by saying that the institution of private property has served to confuse a man with what he possesses, rather than what he is. Thus both elements of a capitalist society, the haves and the have-nots, are crushed, the former by encumbrance and the pursuit of wealth and the latter by starvation. The abolition of private property would free both from the necessity to exist and allow them to live, in the fullest sense of self-realization.

So, for Wilde, socialism is not an end in itself, but a means to the gradual removal of all controls. He is against the authoritarianism of the state as much as he is against the tyranny of the despot. He says that 'all authority is quite degrading. It degrades those who exercise it, and degrades those over whom it is exercised' (*CW* 1182). Most distinctly, in 'The Soul of Man', the assault on authority is an assault on the controls exerted over the artist, for whom he says the best form of government is no government at all. The authority that is most irksome to him is that not of formal censorship, but of public opinion as fostered by journalism: 'what is there behind the leading-article but prejudice, stupidity, cant and twaddle? And when these four are joined together they make a terrible force, and constitute the new authority' (*CW* 1188). The remarks on journalism here have the force of personal experience: Wilde and his novella *The Picture of Dorian Gray* (published in *Lippincott's Magazine* in the previous year) had suffered criticism in precisely the terms of unhealthiness and morbidity that he mentions. Wilde argues that the business of the state is not to dictate the thoughts and actions of the people, only to provide necessary commodities and services, and, in this situation, machinery will undertake all the unfulfilling and undignified labour. The business of the people is likewise not interference in the pursuits of others, but the cultivation of their own individualism of thought and creativity. If the 'state is to make what is useful', the 'individual is to make what is beautiful' (*CW* 1183), and true art will be the guiding principle.

Wilde was not the only, or indeed the first, person to articulate this version of socialism. Grant Allen, who was better known for his controversial novels, had published an essay entitled 'Individualism and Socialism' in the *Contemporary Review* in May 1889. In this he outlined a very similar position to the one suggested by Wilde nearly two years later. Allen argues against the extension of the state and asserts that the free and unimpeded individual should be the basis of the ideal society. 'The Soul of Man' appeared in 1891, in the same issue of *Fortnightly Review* as Allen's 'The Celt in English Art', an article to which Wilde responded with praise and the invitation to inaugurate a 'Celtic Dinner'. Again we can see that Wilde's position is not as idiosyncratic as it might appear, but is firmly embedded in and influenced by the debates of the time.

Wilde's fairy stories, collected as *The Happy Prince and Other Tales* (1888) and *A House of Pomegranates* (1891), also show versions of his political ideas. There is in this perhaps an imitation of his mother, whose collections and retellings of Celtic myth and folk stories had such an impact upon the nascent nationalism of those sections of the Irish people who saw the reclamation of their imaginative heritage as crucial to the assertion of a modern and independent identity. Although Wilde dismissed his stories as slight or simple in some of the letters that accompanied copies of the books that he sent to friends, in one he states directly that they are 'an attempt to mirror modern life in a form remote from reality – to deal with modern problems in a mode that is ideal and not imitative' (L. 388). The stories do bear out many of the theoretical positions that he adopts in 'The Soul of Man'; each of them contains situations of poverty and deprivation, and in many the desperate poverty is juxtaposed with images of incredible wealth and splendour. 'The Young King' is the most obvious of these, in which the new heir discovers through a series of dream visions that the exquisite beauty of his possessions, and especially of the clothing and jewellery being prepared for his coronation, is produced from the misery and suffering of great numbers of his people. He refuses to wear any of the garments, but in the coronation procession he is criticized and rejected by the people: a man steps out of the crowd and demands that the king resume his splendour, because, he says, 'by your pomp we are nurtured, and your vices give us bread' (*CW* 220). The complicity of the poor in their own oppression is revealed for a moment, as is the interest of the established Church in maintaining social inequality, but the story is recuperated at its close into a rather more ordinary message by the universal recognition of the king as a figure of Christian renunciation.

Although some of the other tales, such as 'The Happy Prince', 'The Star Child' and 'The Devoted Friend', initially appear to represent similar situations of renunciation and sacrifice, they also carry the more complex idea that Wilde outlines in 'The Soul of Man' – that Christlike suffering and sacrifice are not necessarily productive of profound social change. The Happy Prince, now a statue, realizes that his beautiful and privileged life has been spent in ignorance of the dreadful conditions of the people and gradually disperses the gold and gems that decorate him to alleviate their state. He and his companion the swallow, who also sacrifices his life, are both received into heaven at the end of the tale, but their suffering is shown to have been a noble waste: the poor are made only temporarily happy and the town councillors squabble over which of them should have a statue of himself cast from the metal of the Prince's figure. In 'The Soul of Man' Wilde argues forcibly that charity is an aggravation of the problem of poverty and that it 'is immoral to use private property in order to alleviate the horrible evils that result from the institution of private property' (*CW* 1174). In a section of the essay that reads with more genuine anger than is usually found in his writing, he criticizes the so-called virtuous poor for acquiescing in their deprivation and professes respect for the 'ungrateful, unthrifty, discontented and rebellious' poor man who refuses to be grateful for the crumbs from the rich man's table when he should be seated at the board. Charity can only ever be a temporary amelioration of the desperate conditions of inequality, and more seriously it serves to perpetuate that inequality by making its conditions just bearable. Charity is a manifestation of that limited sympathy that Wilde identifies with Christian feeling for suffering, and as such he sees that it should have no place in a modern and affluent society like England's, where the available wealth and technological sophistication could eradicate all inequality.

There is a twist that illustrates this at the end of 'The Star Child'. After a long process of suffering and realization of injustice, the Star Child is reunited with his true parents and becomes a benevolent ruler, 'yet ruled he not long, so great had been his suffering, and so bitter the fire of his testing, for after the space of three years he died. And he who came after him ruled evilly' (*CW* 270). Again the message of Christ, of sympathy for others' pain gained through one's own, is shown to be less than complete; charity is a precarious good that rests on the whim of the individual, not the permanent solution to misery and degradation that would come from the abolition of inequality. In 'The Devoted Friend' the prosperous Miller represents himself as the friend of poor Hans, and we recognize the Miller as a harsh depiction of the self-deluded charitable person and Hans as the figure of the virtuous poor. The Miller thinks it best not to invite Hans to his house during the winter because the Miller has food, wine and firewood and does not want Hans, who is starving, to become envious and spoil his fine and uncomplaining nature. The Miller promises Hans his wheelbarrow, and for this act of generosity expects unquestioning gratitude and service. Hans fulfils his service and drowns on an errand for the Miller, who weeps loudly at his funeral. The Miller is not shown to be deliberately conscious of the hypocrisy of his actions, even though he finally acknowledges that the wheelbarrow is useless to him. He believes himself to be acting in a charitable fashion, and that he has a right to expect the fidelity and gratitude of Hans. This belief is so normalized that none of the other people in the story notices the absurdity of the situation and neither does the Water-rat to whom the story is being told.

The story that perhaps comes close to containing an ideal trajectory is also one of the best known, 'The Selfish Giant'.

This can very easily be read as a criticism of private property, and even as an allegory of the Irish situation in which the giant (English) landlord, who has been absent for some time, returns and expels the (Irish) children from his garden. The giant sees the child, who is very obviously the figure of Christ, and is moved to realize the selfishness of his actions. It is important, though, that the giant does not sacrifice himself; he simply realizes that his exclusion of others has been the cause of the bleak emptiness of his garden. As he opens it to the children, they become a community of equals in happiness and enjoyment, a situation that lasts for years and sustains the giant in his old age. At that point the Christ-child reappears to take the old giant to paradise. The Christian message is not negated, but it is not one in which pain and self-sacrifice are necessary; rather the emphasis falls on beauty and pleasure.

It was not only socialism, however idiosyncratic, that Wilde shared with Shaw. Both were Irishmen living and writing in London and had similar opinions on many issues. Amongst many other things, Shaw published attacks on the Criminal Law Amendment Act, stage censorship and Max Nordau's book *Degeneration*. Wilde wrote to Shaw, sending him a copy of *Salome* and praising his article against stage censorship, saying that 'England is a land of intellectual fogs but you have done much to clear the air: we are both Celtic, and I like to think that we are friends' (*L.* 554). Although they did not meet in person more than five or six times, Shaw was a friend and supporter of Wilde. On the day of Wilde's conviction Shaw drafted a petition for his release, but could not gather enough signatures to send it to the Home Secretary.[5]

Wilde's Irish identity is a matter of some contention. It is perhaps the most recent of the identities claimed for him, in the wake of the recognition of Ireland's history in a post-colonial context. Shaw ascribed Wilde's comic talent to his Irishman's perception of English seriousness,[6] but James Joyce rather contemptuously called him the 'court jester to the English'.[7] Terry Eagleton's play *Saint Oscar* (1989) represents Wilde as a rebel against colonial oppression, and more recently Declan Kiberd has placed Wilde very prominently as the first writer of the Irish literary and national revival.[8] Richard Pine also argues very strongly that the fairy stories and tales owe a great deal to the mythical revival in which Lady Wilde was prominent, and that Wilde's first play, *Vera, Or the Nihilists,* is an embodiment of Irish defiance and rebellion and a defence of assassination as a political stratagem.[9] Others have seen Wilde's Irishness as a part of the range of dissident positions that he occupied, in which the principle of difference from the mainstream is of greater significance than the form in which it is expressed. Richard Ellmann's biography argues that Wilde rediscovered his Irish identity on his lecture tour of America. After being criticized in the Irish-American press for 'phrasing about beauty while a hideous tyranny overshadows his native land', he responded very quickly to the presence of Irish-Americans in his lectures and interviews. The Phoenix Park Murders of the Chief Secretary of Ireland and his deputy by extremist Fenians occurred in May of the tour and he replied to a reporter's question that he deplored the violence of the action, but added that England was reaping the fruit of seven centuries of injustice (E. 186). In America he often described himself as a republican, though usually also saying that republics were the most favourable situations for the flourishing of art.

Wilde was certainly living in a period when a variety of different demands for Irish self-government were becoming increasingly vociferous. In the 1870s and 1880s Irish Protestant politicians, most notably Charles Stewart Parnell, tried to gain support for limited self-government, but the controversial Home Rule Bill of 1886 was defeated, despite being backed by Gladstone and the majority of the Liberal Party. Fenians and Nationalists were agitating more strongly for a complete separation of Ireland from English rule, and Unionists were decidedly opposed to any devolution from a British state. An interesting note to this political debate is that Edward Carson, Wilde's contemporary at Trinity College Dublin and adversary in his trials, was among the Unionists, a fact that has been read in support of the suggestion that the courtroom clashes between the two rested on more than simple judicial grounds.[10]

Wilde's family were supporters of Parnell, even though this meant a loss of revenue from their property in Ireland, and Wilde attended the hearings of the Royal Commission set up to investigate allegations against Parnell of incitement to violence. Parnell was disgraced and driven from politics by the revelation of his relationship with a married woman, and it would certainly appear to be Parnell to whom Wilde refers in his attack on the press in 'The Soul of Man', where he writes:

> [they] will drag before the eyes of the public some incident in the private life of a great statesman, of a man who is a leader of political thought as he is a creator of political force, and invite the public to discuss the incident, to exercise authority in the matter, to give their views, and not merely to give their views, but to carry them into action, to dictate to the man upon all other points, to dictate to his party, to dictate to his country; in fact to make themselves ridiculous, offensive and harmful. (*CW* 1189)

Only four years later Wilde would have good cause to apply some of these words to himself.

Wilde's mother was a romantic nationalist whose poetry on mythic subjects and Irish legend had been popular with the 'Young Ireland' movement of the 1840s. She disapproved of Fenian republicanism, and her legacy to her son seems to have been a similarly romantic notion of the Irish people. As in his letter to Shaw, Wilde persistently refers to 'Celts' rather than the Irish: in writing to Gladstone in 1888 he presents him with a copy of *The Happy Prince* and calls Gladstone 'one whom I, and all who have Celtic blood in their veins, must ever honour and revere, and to whom my country is so deeply indebted' (*L.* 350). His country here is clearly Ireland, but in his use of the term 'Celtic' he is including a wider group than just those of Irish nationality. This is obvious in a letter to Grant Allen praising his essay on the Celt in art, where Wilde suggests that '*all* of us who are Celts, Welsh, Scotch and Irish, should inaugurate a Celtic Dinner, and assert ourselves, and show these tedious Angles or Teutons what a race we are, and how proud we are to belong to that race' (*L.* 470). This is, I think, the clue to Wilde's sense of Irish identity: he saw himself much more in racial terms than national. Given his very strong belief in both the existence and the importance of 'the race' as it appears in his evolutionary notions of the development of society through the perfection of the individual, the race that he so frequently refers to in the essays in *Intentions* would seem to be interchangeably the human race in general and the Celtic race in particular. He credits the Celts with recognizable, even stereotyped, characteristics, referring to his own laziness as Celtic (*L*. 689), and seeing them as a rebellious and individualistic people.

This is not to suggest that Wilde saw the Celts only in romantic or mythical terms, because for Wilde, as we have seen in his aesthetic theories, the artistic and imaginative self is not one that is divorced from the possibility of social effect. In another letter, written late in his life, he asserted that 'those who are bringing about Prison Reform in Parliament are Celtic to a man. For every Celt has inborn imagination' (*L*. 1080). The individualistic and imaginative Celt is the ideal politician, because he feels the conditions of the existence of others and can visualize the future situation in which that existence has changed. Having a marginalized identity, the Celt is not one who finds himself degraded by the wielding of authority, but he is also not the type of Wilde's grateful and virtuous poor because of his natural rebelliousness.

Wilde was not only a private sympathizer with radical causes; he was capable of very public actions of allegiance. He strongly supported the cause of the English poet Wilfred Scawen Blunt, who owned property in Ireland but was involved with the Irish Land League, which campaigned for the rights of tenants. Blunt was arrested at a banned meeting in County Galway and sentenced to a prison term. At his appeal the prosecuting counsel was Edward Carson. Blunt wrote a number of poems in prison, published as *In Vinculis*, and Wilde reviewed them very favourably. Wilde's own title for his prison work *De Profundis* (which was Ross's choice) was *Epistola: In Carcere et Vinculis*, echoing Blunt's title and perhaps suggesting that he saw himself as a kind of political prisoner.

Socialism and Irish politics were not the only contemporary controversies in which Wilde took part. The late nineteenth century saw the formation of organized feminist movements, and I want to look now at Wilde's sometimes difficult involvement with women's issues. In 1887 Wilde was invited to become the editor of the *Lady's World*, a monthly periodical that Cassell had already been publishing for a year. In his reply to Thomas Wemyss Reid, Cassell's manager who was probably the anonymous editor of the *Lady's World*, he says that the contents are 'too feminine, and not sufficiently womanly' (*L.* 297), and later appeals for the title to be changed, on the grounds that it has a 'taint of vulgarity about it' and 'will not be applicable to a magazine that aims at being the organ of women of intellect, culture and position' (*L.* 317). Reid agreed and it became the *Woman's World*. Wilde's desire for the change of title and contents suggests more than just an eye for the market. Although he was undoubtedly aware of the changing situation of women in society, this change was by no means complete enough to make a lady's world a thing of the past. Wilde's attitude to women, as suggested through his editorship of the *Woman's World*, is interesting. The magazine contained a wide range of articles over the two years under his direction, and it did largely fulfil his expressed wish to publish 'women's opinions on all subjects of literature, art and modern life' (*L.* 297). Discussion of the 'woman question', the status and higher education of women, professions and work for women all featured repeatedly; and the number of fashion illustrations was reduced and the article on fashion placed last in the magazine. The gossip column of the *Lady's World* disappeared, to be replaced by a section on literary news. Wilde underplays or rejects as unsuitable for women (as opposed to ladies) subjects like gossip and fashion that elsewhere in his writings he elevates to a perverse position of importance. It seems that there is a gendered division here between the frivolous and the serious that reverses the normal expectations. As Laurel Brake notes, 'in this value structure, men are free to be trivial; women are not; men may be useless, and women must be useful'.[11] Wilde edited the *Woman's World* for about twenty issues between November 1887 and October 1889, by which time the list of contributors was flagging and he was losing interest.

The *Woman's World* was not a controversial publication, yet Wilde was retrospectively credited with the creation of the New Woman. In 1895 the *Speaker* claimed that 'the new criticism, the new poetry, even the new woman, are all, more or less, the creatures of Mr Oscar Wilde's fancy',[12] and *Punch* was able to announce in December, six months after Wilde's conviction, 'THE END OF THE NEW WOMAN – The crash has come at last.' In fact, it is hard to see how Wilde might have invented the New Woman. There is almost nothing in his critical writings on any kind of women at all, the tenor of the *Woman's World* was certainly not that of the 'new journalism' and its articles are moderate in their discussions of women's issues. Female characters do appear in the shorter fiction and *The Picture of Dorian Gray*, but are represented in a way that does not challenge the more familiar stereotypes. The *Speaker* article and the *Punch* headline reveal the real grounds for the association of Wilde and the New Woman. The 'at last' of *Punch*'s victory cry indicates a desire for the New Woman to disappear, and Wilde's trials, with their wide but confused publicity of generalized immorality and decadence in gendered terms, provided a convenient moral lesson for any perceived challenge to established notions of gender norms. As in the *Speaker* article, all the 'new', and undesirable, elements are bundled together whatever the reality, or lack of it, in their connections. Wilde's championing of dress reform for women was part of his Aesthetic desire to beautify the environment. The ideal, he said, would be 'a continuation of the Greek principles of beauty with the German principles of health' (*CW* 946), but Aesthetic dress was another victim of the rejection of all the artistic movements with which he had been associated. Wilde was not an outspoken feminist, either in public or in private, and neither did the feminists of the late nineteenth century see him as any kind of ally, either before his trial or after. In fact, after the trials the feminist press was understandably universally critical of him. Their position was embattled enough without being seen to sympathize with a man convicted of sexual deviancy. As Sally Ledger points out, feminism of this period was largely concerned with the control of male sexuality, which was seen as dangerous and oppressive,[13] and Wilde's crime would have been seen by feminists in that continuum, not as a radical challenge to social definitions of gender and sexuality.

A more credible association of Wilde with the New Woman character type rests on the plays. For most of the twentieth century Wilde's reputation as a writer rested on his four society comedies, especially on the last, *The Importance of Being Earnest*. Although it has been suggested that the reason Wilde turned to drama was purely financial, after the poor royalties for *The Picture of Dorian Gray*,[14] two of Wilde's earliest works are plays; *Vera, Or the Nihilists* was finished in 1880 and *The Duchess of Padua* in 1883. Neither was successful, but *The Duchess* was later offered to George Alexander, the new manager of the St James's Theatre. Alexander thought it would cost too much to stage, but gave Wilde a £50 advance for a play on a modern subject. This was *Lady Windermere's Fan*, which opened in 1892 and made Wilde a welcome £7,000 in its first year. Although all four were popular during his lifetime, they were not the most successful dramas of the decade. Kerry Powell's detailed study of the theatre of the 1890s gives a list of the hundred longest runs of plays, and *Lady Windermere's Fan*, *A Woman of No Importance* and *An Ideal Husband* are at number thirty-three, seventy-two and ninety-three respectively. He also argues that Wilde's plays 'depended for life upon dozens of now obscure but once well-known forerunners in the late Victorian theatre'.[15] It has also been suggested that he had little interest in form or innovation in drama, and that he was contemptuous of the avant-garde theatres and theatre clubs, being fixated upon the fashionable theatres like the St James's and flamboyant actor managers like Herbert Beerbohm Tree, who produced *A Woman of No Importance* and *An Ideal Husband*.[16] The critical arguments about Wilde's drama to some extent centre around the questions suggested by these facts, and particularly the arguments as to the range or depth of the social critique contained within them. It has been argued with equal force that the plays are a Trojan horse through which the fashionable audience is exposed to a deep undermining of the values to which they subscribed, or that they represent Wilde's enthralment to that social world and his aspiration to belong to it. There is also the desire, particularly in the case of *Earnest*, to see them as speaking to a double audience, of fashionable society and of a much smaller coterie of homosexual men to whom a coded discourse is intelligible. I shall discuss the question of sexuality in more detail in the next chapter, but here I will look at some aspects of Wilde's drama in the context of the philosophical ideas that have already been outlined, and his participation in contemporary debates about the relations of men and women.

The comedies are conventionally structured well-made plays, and, as Powell points out, they do not represent any formal dramatic innovation, but it is less certain that they were motivated mainly by possible income. The plays do not show such a great difference from Wilde's early work in that they carry over his interest in dialogue as a means of exploring a topic, itself a technique derived from the Greek philosophical dialogues. Both 'The Decay of Lying' and 'The Critic as Artist' are presented as playlets, with an abbreviated dramatis personae and stage directions at their head, and sections of the plays themselves read very much like the exchanges of ideas in the critical pieces, to the extent that passages of the critical essays are actually reproduced in them.

The plays also dramatize Wilde's interest in the multiplicity of personality. The most obvious version of this is, of course, in *Earnest*, where the invented personalities of Bunbury and Earnest become invested with a reality that in Earnest's case is permanent. In the other dramas too there is a range of identities that are more or less invented. In *A Woman of No Importance*, the persona of the widowed Mrs Arbuthnot is adopted by a woman who says that 'one name is as good as another, when one has no right to any name' (*CW* 489), and Lord Illingworth is initially unrecognized by her. To her, he is George Harford, his title being simply the conventional name that signifies the current occupier of a certain estate. On one level, the whole play is, like Earnest, about the contestation of identity, about the name that should be carried, and about the right to confer names upon others, or to refuse them. Illingworth asserts that their son 'is a Harford, every inch of him', but Mrs Arbuthnot counters that she left him because he 'refused to give the child a name' (*CW* 489). Gerald, in writing to his father with the suggestion that Illingworth should marry his mother, agonizes, 'What name can I sign? I who have no right to any name' (*CW* 505). Although the offer of the name is made for both Gerald and Mrs Arbuthnot in Illingworth's proposal, it is refused by them both, and additionally by Hester, although she has earlier referred to 'ruined women' as 'nameless' in a more critical fashion (*CW* 483). The possible identities of 'Gerald Harford' and 'Lady Illingworth' float for a moment in Lord Illingworth's proposal, and in a certain social sense they are actually true, but are rejected; both mother and son prefer the invention of Arbuthnot as representing the people that they have become. The characters of Mrs Erlynne in *Lady Windermere's Fan* and Mrs Cheveley in *An Ideal Husband* are less explicitly but equally invented and convenient labels under which to face the world, but in all cases the name is no longer the disguise that it was when first adopted: it has become the truth of who they are, just as it does with Jack at the end of *Earnest*. It is another example of Wilde's idea of the truth of masks, where one becomes that which one pretends to be, and also of the crude reduction of the multiple personality to a single identity.

There is another implicit renaming in the last scene of *Woman of No Importance*, in which Hester has agreed to marry Gerald and thus will also become Mrs Arbuthnot. In this sense, almost all the female characters have assumed the artificial identities of 'Mrs' or 'Lady'; and those remaining misses, Mabel Chiltern, Gwendolen and Cecily, even Miss Prism, are all poised to join them. It is interesting that the *Woman's World* adopted a mixed practice in naming its contributors, with some appearing simply under their own first and family names with no title, and others, like Wilde's wife Constance, in the most starkly patriarchal form; in Constance's case as 'Mrs Oscar Wilde'.

The debate to which the issue of names for women inevitably alludes is that of marriage, and all four of the society comedies are about marriage. The marriages that will take place at the end of *Woman of No Importance* and *Ideal Husband*, however, are only incidental to the plot. These, and *Lady Windermere's Fan*, are not courtship plays but dramas about the state of marriage. This does reflect the shift in contemporary fiction away from the traditional novel of courtship to more complex depictions of adultery or marital difficulty, and in public debate to the question of the ideal marriage. As the *Westminster Review* noticed in an article, 'Some Modern Ideas about Marriage': 'Periodicals of all descriptions are bursting with them; novels and plays, with and without a purpose, dealing with the many problems that centre around marriage, all springing up with mushroom growth in this and other countries.' The marriage debate was prompted in part by the agitation of feminists for better legal status for women, and by the Married Woman's Property Acts of 1870 and 1888, which had contributed to a growing sense of wives having some right to retain not only their money, but also a sense of themselves as independent beings. Mrs Allonby, in *Lady Windermere's Fan*, says: 'I don't think that we should ever be spoken of as other people's property. All men are married women's property. That is the only definition of what married women's property really is. But we don't belong to anyone' (*CW* 478). In 'The Soul of Man' Wilde has already recognized the function of marriage in capitalist society and the fact that marriage forms another barrier to self-realization; 'with the abolition of private property, marriage in its present form must disappear . . . [Individualism] coverts the abolition of legal restraint into a form of freedom that will make the love of man and woman more wonderful, more beautiful, and more ennobling' (*CW* 1181). These remarks are ambiguously feminist though; in 'The Soul of Man' it is not specifically women to whom he refers, and Mrs Allonby's statement emphasizes, however jokingly, that men become property in marriage too; it is just that they do not realize it. Curiously, marriage in the plays seems to represent constriction and limitation for men, and a kind of protection for women, as though the assumed identity of 'Mrs' allows a freedom that is not available to the single girl. This could be read as a paradoxical reversal of the so-called double standard that was coming under increased criticism by the end of the century. The double standard was the target of the Social Purity campaigns that were a prominent element of late-Victorian feminism. The campaigners argued that higher standards of chastity and moral behaviour were demanded of women, and, rather than loosening these demands, that men too should be expected to conform to them. Although there were a few writers who advocated free love and the celebration of female sexuality, the majority of feminists were not focused on female sexuality at all, except where it was perceived to be an element in their oppression by men, such as in prostitution. The Social Purity campaigns obviously interested Wilde, and it is not surprising to find that he did not agree with them. This was not only because of his own involvement in the sexual subculture, but because the aim was increased state intervention in the lives of individuals, against all that Wilde believed about self-creation and determination. There are many references to the idea in the comedies. In *A Woman of No Importance* Hester is called the Puritan and the MP, Mr Kelvil, is found to have been writing on 'purity' all morning. He asserts that it is 'the one subject of really national importance, nowadays' and goes on to approve of the increasing presence of women in political life, because they 'are always on the side of morality, public and private' (*CW* 469). Of all the female characters in the play, Hester is the only one to appear to meet this standard, but, as we have seen, she reconsiders her position by the end.

Lady Chiltern and Lady Windermere are similar figures, who begin by occupying a rigid and idealistic position that demands moral purity of the kind that Kelvil expresses, and end by recognizing the necessity of adapting their views. The 'good' women are shown to be demanding behaviour from their husbands and enforcing rules upon themselves and others that go against their interests as free individuals. In an exchange between Lady Windermere and Lord Darlington the question of the 'double standard is articulated:

> LORD DARLINGTON. And men? Do you think that there should be the same laws for men as there are for women?
> LADY WINDERMERE. Certainly!
> LORD DARLINGTON. I think life too complex a thing to be settled by these hard and fast rules.
> LADY WINDERMERE. If we had these 'hard and fast rules', we should find life much more simple. (*CW* 423)

Despite the comic tone of the plays, the double standard is not only the subject of jokes: where it is seen in operation it is almost productive of tragedy. This is perhaps most clear in *A Woman of No Importance*, where Mrs Arbuthnot's life is seen to have been very difficult and painful. Mrs Erlynne and Mrs Cheveley are both tinged with a sense of suffering, and in Lady Windermere and Lady Chiltern we see the very narrow escape from what shadow they could have become – outcast women like the others. In *Lady Windermere's Fan* there is a deliberate echo of Thomas Hardy's *Tess of the d'Urbervilles*, published in the previous year, with the subtitle 'A Pure Woman'. Despite the fact that Tess has an illegitimate child and is executed for the murder of its father, Hardy invites the reader to see Tess as a pure woman. Wilde's play has the subtitle 'A Play about a Good Woman' and invites us in similar fashion to consider the nature of the 'goodness' expressed in the play, pressing us further perhaps to identify not Lady Windermere as the good woman, but her mother, Mrs Erlynne. The title of *An Ideal Husband* contains a similar prompt: who, if anyone, is the ideal husband in this play?

In this debate, then, Wilde clearly departs from the contemporary feminist position. Although he is very obviously critical of the double standard, his solution is not to be found in the restriction of masculinity, and certainly not through the kind of state management of the lives of individuals that feminists like Josephine Butler were proposing. In other aspects of his treatment of women too, Wilde seems to reject contemporary ideas. One of these is the role of the mother, and the nature of maternal feeling. An unusual number of Wilde's characters have beautiful, dead mothers with a tragic history (Dorian Gray, the Infanta, the Young King, Cecil Graham in 'The Portrait of Mr W. H.'), but *Lady Windermere's Fan* and *A Woman of No Importance* have quite complex considerations of the question of maternity. Mrs Erlynne is, by social standards, a delinquent mother who has abandoned her daughter in the pursuit of her own desires. Lord Windermere reproaches her: 'A mother's love means devotion, unselfishness, sacrifice' (*CW* 460), but Mrs Erlynne refuses the hard path of public repentance that would reunite her with her child, and chooses to remarry and leave England. She says, 'Only once in my life have I known a mother's feelings . . . they made me suffer . . . I want to live childless still' (*CW* 460), and she rejects suffering and self-sacrifice in favour of individualism. In her actions during the play, however, she has employed the very expectations of the double standard to open her daughter's eyes to the dreadful consequences of subscribing to it. Lord Windermere fails to see it, but she has suffered and sacrificed herself in order that Lady Windermere should not live in either naive puritanism or like her as an outcast. The complexity of Wilde's treatment of the question in this play rescues it from becoming a merely sentimental melodrama. *A Woman of No Importance* is a rather more crude play that comes much closer to sentimentality and melodrama, and this is mainly because of the character of Mrs Arbuthnot. She has none of the attractive attributes of the female dandy seen in Mrs Erlynne, and she appears as the figure of the devoted, unselfish and sacrificing mother that Lord Windermere describes. Her unselfishness is literal, she has no self, and this is a clear suggestion on Wilde's part that the ideal of motherhood requires a woman to give up what he regards as the highest ideal: the cultivation of the individual self. Mrs Arbuthnot's refusal of Illingworth's marriage is not necessarily a bold self-assertion; at the end of the play it seems to be a continued devotion to her martyrdom and a desire to keep her son for herself.

The play in which Wilde seems to show all the characters as achieving the ideal status of self-creation is, of course, *The Importance of Being Earnest*. In this, the self is shown as a fiction, and the competing efforts to be the author of that fiction are exposed. This is particularly apparent in the central character, Jack, confused by his nanny with the manuscript of a novel, and obliged to name himself after the railway station in which he was found. Having been liberated at birth from the troublesome fixity of identity, Jack continues to indulge in the freedom of multiplicity. At his country house he is Jack, but he conjures an imaginary younger, and more disreputable brother, Ernest, whose bad behaviour often obliges Jack to go to London. When in London, however, he assumes the name of Ernest for himself. His friend Algernon equally inventively produces the sickly Bunbury who serves as an all-purpose alibi and excuse for unwelcome occasions. It is not only the men who are allowed the freedom of invention; Cecily chooses to construct an entirely fictional courtship and engagement with Jack's brother, and Gwendolen's determination to love a man called Ernest is based on her imagination of what such a man would be. However, the free play of identity is shown to have its dangers. The invented identities refuse to obey their creators and their existence becomes increasingly real, until it threatens the purposes and even the existence of the other characters. A similar, but tragically rendered, situation can be seen in both *The Picture of Dorian Gray* and 'The Portrait of Mr W. H'. The portraits and the persona of Mr W. H. solidify in their reality, until the only solution is death. Tellingly, it is the invented selves that survive the deaths of their originators. The same is true in Earnest, but the resolution is not death, but marriage. Jack's multiple selves are resolved into one, because he cannot marry Gwendolen unless he satisfies her that he is in fact Ernest, and satisfies Lady Bracknell that he has any name at all. Algernon is able to marry Cecily, having been forced to give up Bunbury, and proved actually to be the younger brother of Jack's that he has been impersonating. Significantly, it is the personalities that the women invent for the men that they are reduced to at the end of the play, and Lady Bracknell who represents the immovable force of the social demand for the singularity of identity.

Despite the political engagement with some contemporary issues concerning women, an oddly conservative sense remains in Wilde's work. This is a sense of women as completely 'other', as almost unknowably different from men. In *Lady Windermere's Fan,* Lord Darlington observes that 'between women and men there is no friendship possible. There is passion, enmity, worship and love, but no friendship' (*CW*439). Whatever the recognition of women as individuals with a right to self-determination that he displays, there seems to be an equally clear recognition that they are a radically different kind of individual. This is expressed most frequently in the social comedies in the form of paradox, where effect is achieved through the inversion of the place or qualities of men and women, but it is more conspicuous in his treatment of two iconic female figures: Salome and the Sphinx. Salome is the archetypal figure of the threatening woman, one that was obsessively represented in art and literature of the period.[17] Wilde's Salome is an independent sexual subject, but this is not the more positive self-determined female dandy of the comedies, but a figure of extreme sexual pathology, as terrifying as the Sphinx in her illogical determination and desire. There is no way to deal with Salome, reason, persuasion and even threat are futile, and the play ends with the chilling command, 'Kill that woman!' (*CW* 605).

The image of the Sphinx, though less well used than Salome, was clearly one that fascinated Wilde. He called his friend Ada Leverson the Sphinx of Modern Life so consistently that there are many letters to her simply addressed 'Dear Sphinx', and he was able to refer to her in this way in letters to other correspondents. There is a more sinister characterization in the long poem 'The Sphinx', where a domestic cat is figured as the terrifying eternal creature who knows and has seen everything. In the poem she has a bloody and pitiless, but fascinating, history of the destruction of men, and Wilde calls her a 'loathsome mystery' that tempts him to be 'what I would not be'. Eventually he summons the image of the crucified Christ to protect him (*CW* 882). She also appears in the short story 'The Sphinx without a Secret', a more comic narrative, in which Gerald falls in love with a mysterious woman. The narrator reassures him that 'women are meant to be loved, not understood' (*CW* 205), but Gerald pursues the woman to a house in a shabby street and, suspecting her of an immoral secret, breaks with her. After her death he discovers that she rented the room and simply sat there alone. The narrator concludes that she was just a woman with a passion for secrecy, a Sphinx without a secret. A trace of the Sphinx can even be seen in a number of the minor female characters in the plays, particularly the domineering and rather terrifying older women. Lady Bracknell is one of these, a figure of monumental fixity who bars Jack's and Algernon's way with a series of apparently unanswerable and arbitrary questions. It would be easy to suggest that this sense of the radical otherness of women is the result, or even the cause, of Wilde's homosexuality, but that would grossly oversimplify both Wilde's own life and work and the complexity of gender relations and sexual identities at the turn of the century. It is to the complexities of sexual identity that we will now turn.

3

Sexuality and the Self

On 18 February 1895 *An Ideal Husband* and *The Importance of Being Earnest* were both being played in the West End and Wilde was staying at a hotel in Piccadilly. That afternoon Lord Alfred Douglas's father, the Marquess of Queensberry, left a calling card at Wilde's club. The writing is very difficult to decipher, but it is generally thought to read 'To Oscar Wilde, posing Sodomite', with the last word misspelled as 'Somdomite'. Wilde picked up the card ten days later, and, although this was not the first time that Queensberry had publicly insulted Wilde, it is this that begins the series of events that was to culminate in Wilde's conviction on seven counts of gross indecency with other male persons and his sentence of two years' imprisonment with hard labour. The events of these three months of Wilde's life are now near-legendary; Douglas's exasperating behaviour; the apparently suicidal decision to sue Queensberry for libel on the basis of the calling card; the exchanges in court with Edward Carson as the opposing counsel; the incriminating testimonies of the young men; Queensberry's acquittal on the libel charge, and the still inexplicable decision on Wilde's part not to leave the country while he had the chance in the hours between the end of the libel trial and his inevitable arrest.

The trials and conviction were calamitous, and not just for Wilde. His family were deeply affected. His wife Constance lived up to her name. She wrote to him frequently, she visited him in prison to break the news of his mother's death, she never divorced him and against advice from her friends provided an allowance for him after his release. Although they discussed meeting again, they never did, and she died two years before Wilde, in 1898. Wilde's elder son Cyril felt his father's disgrace keenly and expressed his desire to perform heroic and manly actions in expiation. At the outbreak of the First World War he volunteered and was killed in combat. The conviction also effectively crushed the wider culture of Aestheticism with which he had been associated. Its main journal, *The Yellow Book,* was deserted by its contributors and closed, unsurprisingly given the general condemnation of all that Wilde was seen to represent. He was living proof of the decadence of art and culture and a bleak example to many others. The *National Observer*'s leading article said: '. . . to the exposure [of Wilde] there must be legal and social sequels. There must be another trial at the Old Bailey, or a coroner's inquest – the latter for choice; and of the Decadents, of their hideous conceptions of the meaning of Art, of their worse than Elusinian mysteries, there must be an absolute end.'[1] It is said that on the night of Wilde's conviction it was impossible to get a seat on the boat train as scores of young men fled to the Continent to escape prosecution. Whatever the truth of this, the trials and conviction had, and continued to have, a profound effect on issues of sexuality and gender long after Wilde's death. In this chapter I will discuss Wilde's place in the debates about sexuality and morality that occupied such a great deal of attention in the *fin de siècle* and look at four of his works, *The Picture of Dorian Gray, De Profundis,* 'Pen, Pencil and Poison' and 'The Portrait of Mr W. H.' as examinations of some of the issues.

It is difficult to locate Wilde in the context of gender and sexuality in the late nineteenth century. The 'Woman Question' of mid-century had, by the 1880s, generated a range of significant social and legal changes, and the debates had grown more rather than less intense as the slow effects of these changes began to be felt in society. Although, as noted in the previous chapter, it has been argued that the New Woman was largely a creation of the journalism and fiction of the time,[2] women were certainly to be seen in increasing numbers in the places of education, science, work and political organization. Simultaneously, if in less obviously dramatic ways, ideas, practices and representations of masculinity were shifting too. This is not to say that there was a sudden destabilizing of gender categories from a position of relative fixity. Ideologies of gender had never been quite as simple as a division of qualities and their distribution across male and female bodies. Although a certain simplicity of gender roles is often suggested, those general notions of the places of men and women in the mid-nineteenth century are complicated by the various fissures produced by elements such as class, education, race or geographical location and it is the case that the last decades of the century rather saw an intensification both of change in images of gender and of the anxiety associated with it. The difficulty in locating Wilde lies in the fact that he was to some extent part of the impulse of those changes, as well as being the most famous casualty of those anxieties.

In many ways Wilde has become one of the defining principles by which we have come to understand issues of gender, and more particularly issues of sexuality. Thus his place is complicated by our contemporary view. As Alan Sinfield comments, 'our interpretation is retroactive; in fact, Wilde and his writings look queer because our stereotypical notion of male homosexuality derives from Wilde, and our ideas about him'.[3] Because of this it becomes tricky to disentangle Wilde from his legacy and to see him as he was seen at the time, and by himself. I am certainly not suggesting that it is possible to recover a 'real' Wilde, free from the subsequent interpretations of him, nor to discard what Wilde came to mean, because that in itself is very important in revealing the ways in which sexuality was understood in the twentieth century. However, in untangling Wilde's contemporary situation we can perhaps see him as representing possibly the last figure of a kind particular to the nineteenth century, rather than the first of a kind particular to the twentieth. For example, it is only just possible to use the term 'homosexuality' with any historical accuracy in relation to this period. The word had been used in German, probably for the first time in 1869, but it was by no means in common usage in English, even by the 1890s. Wilde never used it, and nor did many of his contemporaries, who, struggling after a vocabulary, preferred either more classically derived terms, like Uranian, or more scientific terminology, such as 'homogenic' or inversion.

Anxieties about sexuality were fuelled from a number of sources, and the Criminal Law Amendment Act of 1885 under which Wilde was prosecuted is a good example of the knot of ideas around sexuality. It dealt mainly with women, outlawing brothel keeping and the procurement of women for prostitution, and raising the age of consent for girls to 16. It also contained Section 11, better known as the Labouchère Amendment, a last-minute addition to the Bill, which introduced a new category of offence: gross indecency between male persons, specifying that this offence could be committed in public or private. This mixed piece of new legislation was the outcome of several different campaigns of the type discussed in the previous chapter that were concerned with public and private morality. It was pushed through at this particular time primarily in response to sensationalist press accounts of 'white slavery', not least W. T. Stead's infamous 'Maiden Tribute of Modern Babylon' articles in the *Pall Mall Gazette*, where he claimed to have purchased a 13-year-old virgin for £5. The Act was supported by feminists, many of whom had been part of other campaigns to protect women and girls and to help those working in prostitution. Labouchère's late amendment seems also to have resulted from Stead's work. He stated that his motive in proposing the amendment was his response to a report on male prostitution that Stead had sent him.[4]

The Act itself serves as a good illustration of Michel Foucault's influential analysis of the history of sexuality, where he writes of the formation in this period of what he calls the 'four great strategic unities which . . . formed specific mechanisms of knowledge and power centring on sex'[5] and brought what had been ostensibly private matters within the detailed governance of law, medicine and education. The first of these he calls the hysterization of women's bodies, in which the feminine body was seen as saturated with sexuality, and therefore a necessary object of control, particularly medical. The second is the ambiguous assertion that practically all children are prone to indulge in sexual activity, and that this sexual activity, doubly characterized as 'natural' and 'unnatural', posed physical, moral, individual and collective dangers. The third is the socialization of procreative behaviour through the absorption of marriage into economic and medical structures, and the last is the psychiatrization of perverse pleasure, in which the sexual instinct was isolated as a separate biological and psychical instinct, and assigned a role of normalization or pathologization in relation to all aspects of an individual's behaviour. Foucault argues that the isolation of the sexual instinct as a separate and defining characteristic led to the proliferation of 'perverse' sexualities, as the new profession of sexology constructed a range of them through its efforts at definition. The corollary of this is the production of the notion of the possible correction of sexual anomalies through psycho-medical intervention.

The problem in locating Wilde is that he is so intricately enmeshed in this. Indeed, he further illustrates Foucault's point that there is no simple imposition of power on a group who are passive and powerless, but that the operations of power necessarily include all individuals in an active capacity. Wilde is typical in that he exploits some of the familiar discourse of decadence for his own ends, but in becoming emblematic of it for others makes himself vulnerable to its implications. Max Nordau in his highly popular book *Degeneration* (1895) calls Wilde the chief of the Aesthetes,[6] but his description of him is in many ways no different from the ways in which Wilde had presented himself; Nordau just draws different conclusions. Wilde then becomes the most celebrated defendant under the terms of the legislation, itself an event that seems to have been an unforeseen consequence of the Criminal Law Amendment Act. Of the principal architects of the Act, Henry Labouchère was a friendly acquaintance of both Oscar and Constance, and Stead maintained afterwards that he had not joined in or relished the hounding of Wilde.[7]

Foucault's well-known analysis of the epistemes of sexuality seems nowhere more applicable than it does to Wilde:

> This new persecution of the peripheral sexualities entailed an incorporation of perversions and a new specification of individuals . . . The nineteenth-century homosexual became a personage, a past, a case history, and a childhood, in addition to being a type of life, a life form and a morphology with an indiscreet anatomy and possibly a mysterious physiology. Nothing that went into his total composition was unaffected by his sexuality. It was every-

> where present in him: at the root of all his actions because it was their insidious and indefinitely active principle; written immodestly on his face and body because it was a secret that always gave itself away . . . The sodomite had been a temporary aberration; the homosexual was now a species.[8]

Whereas same-sex relations had always occurred, they were not considered to be defining, or even recurring, characteristics of an individual. After the end of the nineteenth century such actions were seen to be one of the principal and permanent definitions of a person's identity. It almost seems possible to locate Wilde in the precise moment that this occurs in Britain. It is after, and arguably through, Wilde that the 'species' of homosexual becomes clearly identified in law and medicine, as well as in the popular imagination, with his name as its shorthand title. In E. M. Forster's *Maurice*, the title character, attempting to discuss his situation with a doctor, says that he is 'an unspeakable of the Oscar Wilde sort'.[9] The contemporary sexologist Havelock Ellis included in his book *Sexual Inversion* the comment: 'The Oscar Wilde trial, with its wide publicity, and the fundamental nature of the questions it suggested, appears to have generally contributed to give definiteness and self-consciousness to the manifestations of homosexuality, and aroused inverts to take up a definite attitude.'[10] This remark suggests something further than the simple labelling of sexual unorthodoxy by those in power, and something closer to Foucault's description of the 'reverse discourse', in which those labelled take up the title in more or less militant self-identification.

The issue of sexuality is further complicated by issues of gender, and particularly in Wilde's case with the idea of effeminacy. Alan Sinfield argues very convincingly that Wilde's trials mark the moment when an older idea of effeminacy, which had not been exclusively identified with same-sex relationships, was compressed together with homosexuality. Effeminacy had meant womanish and having a woman's weak sense of morality (so therefore also liable to debauchery and not exclusive of homosexual behaviour), but it had also described men who spent too much time with women and as such were identified as adulterers and heterosexual philanderers. Effeminacy was also associated with dandyism, and versions of these elements can be seen in much earlier writings – in Restoration comedies, for example. In William Wycherley's *The Country Wife*, the rake Horner is vain in his personal appearance, makes witty quips like the Wildean dandy and has a rumour of impotence put about to facilitate his (heterosexual) affairs. There are comparisons to be made between the Restoration rakes and Wilde's plays in which figures like Lord Darlington in *Lady Windermere's Fan*, or Lord Goring in *An Ideal Husband*, seem to represent quite clearly an older idea of effeminacy that includes dandyism and more heterosexually oriented philandering. Wilde's own dandyism was very consciously adopted as part of his Aesthetic persona, and it also marks out a class aspiration. This too was later to prove problematic for Wilde. Class relations were among the other anxieties articulated at the trial, and at least part of the difficulty was the perceived inappropriateness of the mainly working-class young men as companions of any kind to a man of Wilde's status. So, although his dandyism derived from an older model, effeminacy, homosexuality and the predatory exploitation of vulnerable younger and poorer men were previously separate things collapsed together in and around Wilde's trials to form a new image of the homosexual man.

If effeminacy precedes and overlaps with homosexuality in this way, and the Aesthete was not necessarily seen as homosexual, then it is important to ask how Wilde was understood by his contemporaries. Ed Cohen's book on the trials centres on the question of what was known. He says that at no time did the newspapers describe or even directly refer to the charges made against Wilde.[11] Although it has come to be thought that the public always knew that Wilde was behaving dangerously and that the trials merely exposed what 'everyone' already knew, this appears not to be the case. A number of people who recorded their recollections of Wilde said that they had had no idea until the charges were made. Amongst Wilde's friends, Frank Harris claimed that he knew nothing – 'I did not know. I did not believe the accusation. I did not believe it for a moment'[12] – until he was disabused of his innocence in a conversation with Wilde. Although Harris is widely regarded as an unreliable source, this also may be the episode that Wilde himself describes in *De Profundis* (*CW*

1050). Lucy Bland quotes the writer and feminist Evelyn Sharp, who contributed to *The Yellow Book* and knew Aubrey Beardsley, and who might therefore be expected to have some knowledge of sexual unorthodoxy, as saying that homosexuality was 'something of which I, in common, I believe, with numbers of my contemporaries, were entirely ignorant until the Oscar Wilde trial set everybody talking about in corners'.[13] On the other hand, there is George Bernard Shaw who attacked both Labouchère and his amendment when a raid on a transvestite brothel in central London was reported in Labouchère's own journal, *Truth*. Shaw not only demanded the repeal of the Amendment, but also dismissed hypocritical claims of ignorance:

> Now I do not believe myself to be the only man in England acquainted with these facts. And I strongly protest against any journalist writing, as nine out of ten are at this moment dipping their pens to write, as if he has never heard of such things except as vague and sinister rumours concerning the most corrupt phases in the decadence of Babylon, Greece and Rome.[14]

Whatever the level of knowledge of homosexuality that existed elsewhere in society, the central person about whom the question 'what did everyone know' can be asked is Wilde himself.

He appears to have shown little interest either in the work on sexology that was beginning to be published or in the nascent campaigns around homosexuality, all of which would have been easily accessible to him. Wilde knew both Edward Carpenter and John Addington Symonds, who were among the most outspoken of scholars and agitators for recognition of same-sex relations. Symonds and his work he knew well; he writes of reviewing Symonds's book *Studies of the Greek Poets* in 1876 (*L.* 31), and both men served briefly on the Council of the Hellenic Society. A book by Symonds appears on each of the lists of books that Wilde requested in prison. Both Symonds and Carpenter seem to offer possible theoretical or political positions to Wilde. Carpenter published three pamphlets on 'sex-love' in 1894, as well as privately circulating his essay on 'homogenic' love. He was a socialist who believed that new forms of sexual and emotional relationship would arise from socialism and true democracy, and his community at Milthorpe, where he later lived openly with his lover George Merrill, was a testament to this. Carpenter was influenced by American Transcendentalists such as Emerson and Whitman (both of whom Wilde also met on his American tour) and argued that union and not procreation was the highest object of sex, and that sex, including homosexuality, was not necessarily sexual at all in terms of physical acts but represented transcendent love.

There continues to be a vigorous debate about the existence or otherwise of what could be called a homosexual community in the last decades of the nineteenth century. There is obviously a network of some kind operating in relation to the sex trade, and there were certainly individual scholars and cautious campaigners and some looser groups in the academic and cultural sphere. *The Artist and Journal of Home Culture* under the editorship of Charles Jackson and *The Studio* under his friend Joseph White were publishing some polemical and research articles on homosexuality, as well as poetry and fiction. At Oxford, *The Spirit Lamp* was edited by Douglas in his final year there, and published contributions from Symonds, Wilde and Robert Ross. Another publication, *Chameleon*, produced its one and only issue in late 1894. It contained a piece by Wilde, but it was the story 'The Priest and the Acolyte' by the magazine's editor, with its clearly depicted sexual relationship between two men, that caused outrage and was cited at Wilde's trial. Even Alfred Douglas appeared more militant in the cause, and after Wilde's sentencing wrote to Stead and Labouchère (both were editors of journals), mentioning a pamphlet by Krafft-Ebing that called for the repeal of Austrian laws on homosexuality, and pointing out the tolerance of sexual difference afforded under the French legal system. Neither man published the letters.

If there was a homosexual 'community', Wilde does not seem to have belonged to it. His participation in the sex trade is not doubted, but this was a very loosely organized network that contained a significant proportion of young men who saw it only as a means to an income through prostitution or blackmail. Wilde's involvement in this network does not appear to have produced a sense of identification with other men for whom sexuality was a defining feature of their lives. Frank Harris describes Wilde as being surrounded by a band of 'passionate admirers' who were 'mostly sexual inverts',[15] though this does not really accord with his claim to have been convinced of Wilde's innocence of the charges. Wilde also knew George Ives, who founded the homosexual secret society of the Order of Chaeronea in 1893, and there are letters from Wilde to Ives dating from that year, but the evidence suggests that it is unlikely he belonged to it. There are some interesting letters to Ives after his release from prison. In these later letters he chides Ives for his secrecy and calls him a 'great baby' (*L.* 1172), but in the last he refers to Edward Carpenter's *Civilization, Cause and Cure,* calling it 'most suggestive' (*L.* 1197). The only time that Wilde refers to 'we' in a context that could mean a homosexual community or an identification of himself with other homosexual men is in a letter to Ives in 1898, where he says: 'Yes: I have no doubt that we shall win, but the road is long and red with monstrous martyrdoms. Nothing but the repeal of the Criminal Law Amendment Act would do any good. That is the essential. It is not so much public opinion as public officials that need educating' (*L.* 1044).

If communes or secret societies were not to Wilde's taste, the apparent evasion of Symonds is less explicable. He would seem far closer to Wilde: both were married with children, both were Oxford graduates and classical scholars with a particular interest in Greek. Symonds had been a student of Jowett's at Balliol and one of the most troubled of Jowett's followers. To the distress of some of his students, Jowett had translated the 'spiritual procreancy' of the Platonic relationship between men into the carnal procreancy of bourgeois marriage and decried sexual and erotic relations between men as unnatural. Symonds had a bitter break from Jowett, and went on to write two books on the specific issue of sexuality. He produced ten copies of the first, *A Problem in Greek Ethics,* in 1883 (with the subtitle 'An Inquiry into the Phenomena of Sexual Inversion Addressed especially to Medical Psychologists and Jurists'), and the second, *A Problem in Modern Ethics,* he produced (with a similar subtitle) in a run of fifty copies in 1891. In both he appeals to history as an alternative to law, psychiatry and forensic medicine in understanding homosexuality, and he actually uses that term in *Greek Ethics*, though he adopts 'inversion' in *Modern Ethics*, preferring it as a title 'found by Science'. Symonds also worked with Havelock Ellis, the foremost of the new British sexologists, on the production of *Sexual Inversion*, which was in fact a joint project, although, after Symonds had died in 1893, and after Wilde's trials, Symonds's family pressed Ellis to expunge Symonds's name.

Symonds, in *Greek Ethics*, identifies a 'base form of paederastia', which he says 'does not vary to any great extent, whether we observe it in Athens or in Rome, in Florence of the sixteenth century or in Paris of the nineteenth century'.[16] He then goes on to detail a nobler type that he calls Greek love, which is 'a passionate and enthusiastic attachment subsisting between man and youth, recognized by society and protected by opinion, which, though it was not free from sensuality, did not degenerate into mere licentiousness'.[17] In an attempt to locate this type of relationship historically, he surveys a number of instances and comments: 'A considerable majority of the legends which have been related in the previous section are Dorian, and the Dorians gave the earliest and most marked encouragement to Greek love.'[18] It is hard to believe that the name of Dorian Gray is coincidental.

Symonds goes further in *A Problem in Modern Ethics*. The title makes clear the link with the earlier work and he presents it as a discussion of a question that is pressing in contemporary society, with its greater knowledge of evolutionary science and the 'risk' of any family 'producing a boy or girl whose life will be embittered by inverted sexuality'.[19] In this later work he lists a number of 'vulgar errors' about homosexuality: that homosexuals are depraved; that sodomy is the single object of same-sex desire; that young boys are liable to corruption; and that homosexuals are easily identifiable on the basis of their appearance and manner.[20] He catalogues several types of homosexuality, including forced abstinence from women; 'curious seeking after novel pleasure'; pronounced morbidity; historical epochs where the habit is nationally established and then 'those who behave precisely like persons of normal sexual proclivities, display no signs of insanity, and have no morbid constitutional diathesis to account for their peculiarity'.[21] All of which leads him to conclude that sexual inversion is not an appropriate subject for legislation. On the publication of *The Picture of Dorian Gray* in *Lippincott's Magazine* in 1890, Symonds wrote to a friend, Horatio Brown: 'It is an odd and audacious production, unwholesome in tone, but artistically and psychologically interesting. If the British public will stand this, they can stand anything. However I resent the unhealthy, scented, mystic, congested touch which a man of this sort has on moral problems.'[22] Despite its debts to the kinds of Greek models that Symonds outlines, Wilde's novel is clearly not entirely in accord with Symonds's position. Oddly, the last sentence in the quotation sounds much closer to the hostile reviews that followed the novel's publication. Perhaps for Symonds there is the contrast that Wilde had expressed in 'Hélas!' in which the 'austere control' of the beloved Greek culture is thought to have given way to distorted Paterian self-indulgence. 'A man of this sort' is an interesting characterization, and an obvious distancing on Symonds's part from someone who otherwise appears to be very similar. Symonds picks up the language of degeneration in his use of words like unwholesome and unhealthy, and these were the ways in which homosexuality was generally and euphemistically voiced, although it was still not an exclusive identification, and 'unhealthiness' was often mixed up with other rather more heterosexual ideas, such as contraception.

Wilde always refused any characterization of his work as unhealthy. In the newspaper correspondence after *Dorian Gray* he persistently attempts to shift the argument to the issue of aesthetics, as he did when he was questioned about his writing and his letters in court. He similarly refused any description of himself as morally unhealthy. This was not because he was afraid of the consequences of doing so; he simply believed that it was not true. The only times in which Wilde acknowledges his sexuality in the same terms as the courts or critics are the petitions to the Home Secretary for his early release. He writes in *De Profundis* that 'Reason . . . tells me that the laws under which I am convicted are wrong and unjust laws, and the system under which I have suffered a wrong and unjust system. But somehow, I have got to make both of these things just and right to me' (*CW* 1020). This was not an effort to acquiesce to the law, but part of his belief in the progress of the self through the assimilation of experience. He obviously did not wish to remain in prison and recognized that the only way in which he might secure release would be to appeal on the same medical/psychiatric grounds that stood behind the legal form of his crime, having failed so signally to convince the judge, jury or the general public of his innocence in his own terms. He never repeats in any other context the pathological description that he employs in the appeals, but it is interesting that he is able to do so here, showing as it does his familiarity with the discourse.

In the first appeal in July 1896 he speaks of 'the terrible offences of which he was rightly found guilty' and appeals to the scientific versions of them: 'Such offences are forms of sexual madness and are recognized as such not merely by modern pathological science, but by much modern legislation' (*L*. 656). He develops the notion of insanity associated with the artistic temperament that Nordau made popular, and goes on to speak of his fear that the insanity that had produced 'monstrous sexual perversion' would extend and destroy all his sanity. In his second petition of November 1896 he writes:

> Of all modes of insanity – and the petitioner is fully conscious now, too conscious it may be, that his whole life, for the two years preceding his ruin, was the prey of absolute madness – the insanity of perverted sensual instinct is the one most dominant in its action on the brain. It tints the intellectual as well as the emotional energies. It clings like a malaria to soul and body alike. (*L*. 667)

This is very different from his speech in the second trial where he defends loving relationships between men, which he says are:

> Such a great affection of an elder for a younger man, as there was between David and Jonathan, such as Plato made the very basis of his philosophy, and such as you find in the sonnets of Michaelangelo and of Shakespeare. It is that deep, spiritual affection that is as pure as it is perfect. It dictates and pervades great works of art . . . It is beautiful, it is fine, it is the noblest form of affection. There is nothing unnatural about it. It is intellectual, and it repeatedly exists between an elder and a younger man, when the elder has intellect and the younger man has all the joy and hope and glamour of life before him. (E. 435)

This is very close to Symonds's characterization of paederastia, and is not simply Wilde's desperate attempt to avoid the conviction that by then looked inevitable. It is formed entirely out of the lineage of his Greek studies and the tracing of that lineage through to the present, as Pater had done implicitly in *The Renaissance*. He seeks the same vindication of tradition, and after his release he defiantly maintained the position he had held all his life. In a letter to Robert Ross in February 1898 he repeats the declaration he made in court: 'A patriot put in prison for loving his country loves his country, and a poet in prison for loving boys loves boys. To have altered my life would have been to have admitted that Uranian love is ignoble. I hold it to be noble – more noble than other forms' (*L.* 1019). In these remarks to Ross, Wilde still appears to regard homosexuality as acquired, and even as consciously chosen, behaviour.

Earlier, in fact at the same time as the second appeal to the Home Secretary but in rather different language, he had written, also to Robert Ross: 'Do not think that I would blame [Douglas] for my vices. He had as little to do with them as I had with his. Nature was in this matter a stepmother to each of us';[23] and later in the same letter: 'I am utterly ashamed of my friendship with [Douglas]. For by their friendships men can be judged. It is a test of every man. And I feel more poignant abasement of shame . . . fifty thousand times more . . . than I do, say, for my connection with Charley Parker' (*L.* 670). His 'nature' it seems is an inborn quality, but his performance of it is within his own will. As with his comment about Parker, who was one of the young men who gave evidence against him, what consistently emerges in his letters is his lack of shame at the specific charges. In June 1897 he writes: 'I really am not ashamed of having been in prison. I am thoroughly ashamed of having led a life quite unworthy of an artist. I do not accept the British view that Messalina is better than Sporus: these things are matters of temperament, and both are equally vile, because sensual pleasures wreck the soul' (*L.* 879). He criticizes the differential treatment of sexual misconduct where Messalina, who is emblematic of perverse but female hetero-sexual promiscuity, should be less censured than Sporus, who represents male same-sex relations.

Wilde does express shame, but never for sexual misconduct. His shame comes from different sources, and for this there is some explanation in his work. His reassessment of his relationship with Douglas shows his regret to lie in the loss of the driving purpose of his life, the perfection of individuality. He constantly reiterates his loss of selfhood, writing in *De Profundis*: 'I blame myself for allowing an unintellectual friendship to dominate my life' (*CW* 981), and describes his 'ethical degradation' and his 'will-power absolutely subject' to Douglas (*CW* 984). What this loss of self led him to was, among other things, his 'feasting with panthers', the sexual encounters with working-class young men. Again, it is not the relationships, or the sexual content of them, that he regrets, but the fact that they were unconsidered, and unredeemed by any art or aesthetic morality. His description in *De Profundis* of his participation in 'the imperfect world of coarse uncompleted passions, of appetite without distinction, desire without limit, and formless greed' (*CW* 1014) is in the language of an art critic. He uses words like incomplete and imperfect and formless, as though he is ashamed of the aesthetic quality of his actions, and he speaks of distinction as a discriminatory judgement that is lacking. These were ugly relationships, not because they were wrong in the sense that the court contended, but because they were without critical discrimination and represented the mere indulgence of sense, a stagnant activity without progress.

De Profundis recognizes sin and repentance, or, perhaps more accurately, error and realization of error, but these are not new ideas for Wilde. In his characterization of them in the prison letter he does not alter his conception of sin and repentance; rather it seems he comes to understand them in relation to his own life and art, and not as abstractions. The 'crimes' that Wilde acknowledges in *De Profundis* are his own transgressions against truth, beauty and the duty to art; in much the same way as he does in 'Pen, Pencil and Poison', when he more humorously identifies Wainewright's 'crime' not as the poisoning of several people, but his awful influence on the writing style of journalists. The refusal to recognize it as a sin is not a conviction of the rightness of his actions; he recognizes wrongness but in an entirely different paradigm. The misunderstanding of his actions or writings is the misunderstanding of the artistic nature of his motivation; his shame is at his failure to meet the standards of his art.

The Picture of Dorian Gray is not any kind of provocation to the limitless indulgence of desire, but a testament to the difficulty of living by one's artistic principles. *Dorian Gray* and *De Profundis* are texts about failure, as are 'Pen, Pencil and Poison' and 'The Portrait of Mr W. H.'. If anything, *The Picture of Dorian Gray*, and even more strongly *De Profundis*, are recognitions of the difficulty of living in the dialectical mode that is his ideal, and recognizing the actions that can be seen as contributing to the 'becoming' of the individual. These texts are lamentations of the failure of the ideal of Greek love, of the artistic personality, of the proper discernment of the critic, and ultimately of the individuated self. The failures in *Dorian Gray* are seen in Basil because of the domination of personality, in Dorian because of the mere sinking into the pleasure of perverse sensations, and in Lord Henry because of his refusal to engage with life. In *De Profundis* Wilde casts himself as a hybrid of Basil and Dorian, using exactly the same terms of definition as he has used in *Dorian Gray*. *The Picture of Dorian Gray* is the text most frequently read (perhaps alongside *Earnest* as a comic version) as an uncanny prefiguring of the disastrous relationship with Lord Alfred Douglas, although he did not meet Douglas until 1891, the year after its publication. The novel was certainly treated as solid evidence of his 'sodomitical tendencies' in his trials, and the arguments that Wilde engaged in with the opposing barrister, Edward Carson, were recapitulations of his dismissal of accusations against the novel at the time of its first publication in *Lippincott's Magazine* in June 1890. This magazine version, which differed in some respects from the single-volume publication, would have been the version most readers were familiar with. Stuart Mason says that the 1,000 copies of the first edition of the single-volume version took five years to sell,[24] and indeed there was confusion at the trial with different people having different versions in front of them.

There are several reasons why *The Picture of Dorian Gray* is read as a prescient tale. One is the suggestion elsewhere in Wilde's work, especially in 'Lord Arthur Savile's Crime', of the prediction of the crime actually producing it, but the major reason is, I think, that significant sections of *De Profundis* work as a rereading of the relationship with Douglas in terms that are very close to those of *Dorian Gray*. It seems that Wilde reread himself in terms of his fiction, and I would suggest that his identification with the novel was probably rather closer during his imprisonment than it was at the time that he wrote it. Wilde's self-examination in prison takes place in relation to a number of books. He turned again to the practice of keeping a notebook of his reading, as he had at Oxford, and he commented on the importance of doing so and the pleasure that it gave him. Although he was not allowed copies of his own works in prison, he could obviously recall them, and many sections of *De Profundis* echo passages of *Dorian Gray*, not just because Wilde could never let a good line go, or because he still depended on the structures of thought he had erected at Oxford (though both these things are also true), but because, as he says in *De Profundis*, he came to see himself as the actor in a tragedy rather than in a brilliant comedy (*CW* 998). This is not to suggest that *De Profundis* is a tragic version of *Dorian Gray*, because the latter is a tragedy too, even if contemporary critics did not see it in that way.

Wilde took part in several exchanges of published correspondence after *Dorian Gray*'s publication. The *Scots Observer* review is typical, if a little more outspoken than some: 'it is false art – for its interest is medico-legal . . . matters only fitted for the Criminal Investigation Department or a hearing *in camera* . . . he can write for none but outlawed noblemen and perverted telegraph boys.'[25] This obviously shows the terms on which that reviewer understood it. It is the most direct reference among a number of reviews that suggested its general unwholesomeness, and is the review that Carson chose to refer to in the libel trial. Wilde's defence of *Dorian Gray* in the correspondence pages of the *St James's Gazette*, the *Daily Chronicle* and the *Scots Observer* insists that the atmosphere of 'moral corruption' is 'vague and indeterminate' and that 'each man sees his own sin in Dorian Gray' (*L.* 439). Most critics had little problem in identifying the atmosphere as 'unhealthy', and, although most stopped short of a direct accusation of homosexuality, the *Scots Observer* piece made suggestive reference to the figures of outlawed noblemen and perverted telegraph boys familiar from the Cleveland Street transvestite brothel scandal. Edward Carson in the libel trial certainly did not stop short of such an accusation and pressed Wilde into an admission that it could be read as 'sodomitical', and that in response to Walter Pater's misgivings on that account he had amended the text between the publication of *Lippincott*'s version and the book. The passage of Basil's confession that had talked of never having loved a woman and adoring Dorian 'madly, extravagantly and absurdly' dropped those statements and was altered to read more specifically as the pursuit of Platonic artistic ideals.

Carson was attempting to defend Queensberry against the accusation of libel, so it is not surprising that he resorted to the terms of the charge, specifically the 'sodomite' terminology of Queensberry's card. What is interesting here is that both Carson and Wilde fall into a usage of that term to mean more generally the type of relationship of 'gross indecency' named by the Labouchère Amendment, even though part of the point of it was that it was no longer necessary to prove a specific act of sodomy to secure a conviction for the new crime of gross indecency. As in Foucault's analysis, this is no longer about actions so much as the extended 'atmosphere' of homosexuality. The deliberate vagueness of the moral corruption of *Dorian Gray* is problematic. Far from each man seeing his own sin in the novel, most have preferred to see Wilde's, either as Carson did, or more recently and more positively as a coded treatment of homosexuality. In either reading it is hard to fit the novel across the grid of coded sexual identity that is imagined to exist. At the same time as making the identifications of sodomitical tendencies, the accusers, or latterly those wishing to see homosexual manifestos in his work, have to read across and ignore the explicitly heterosexual relationships that exist in the novel. The most obvious is Dorian's with Sybil Vane, and Basil also mentions Dorian's disgracing of Henry's sister Gwendolen. I agree here with Sinfield, Bristow and others that the heterosexual relationships are not a screen for the novel 'really' being about homosexuality, but in fact that the confusion of possible readings represents a crucial point in history at which the discourses that make that kind of simple identification of a person as one or the other, as heterosexual or homosexual, are in the process of being settled. The image of the dandy as a danger to women also persists in this, and it is easy to see the coalescing of the images of dandy, effeminate man and predatory homosexual that Alan Sinfield discusses. As Wilde had said in 'Pen, Pencil and Poison', the law does solve the subtle problem of the permanence of personality in a rough-and-ready manner, and in Wilde's own case, as well as that of *Dorian Gray*, both the law and the critics proved unable to deal with the multiple and dialectical self that Wilde tried to be and tried to represent in his characters. They preferred to reduce it to the single figure of the immoral sexual degenerate.

It is not only in the trial that Wilde was arguing from a very different understanding of morality; he is already struggling to assert it in the debate that followed the publication of *Dorian Gray*. He said in his correspondence with the reviewers that what he thought was too obvious in the book was its moral, that 'all excess, as well as all renunciation, brings its punishment', yet he means the message of the book rather than the moral as the critics chose to understand the term. He also said that the novel 'does not enunciate its law as a general principle, but realizes itself purely in the lives of individuals' (*L.* 435). This is the key to understanding his defence and his work, because for Wilde there can be no fixed principle, individuation is the highest law, necessary to stimulate and contribute to change in people and in society.

The novel places the reader in an uncomfortable position, because there is a sense of a strong message being contained in it at the same time that there seems to be a wilful refusal on Wilde's part to give clues as to where, or in whom, to locate it. The distribution of roles is unclear, it is without heroes or villains and suggests that all the characters are both victims and in some way culpable. There is no clear way of identifying with the characters or singling out a moral stance. Basil is a rather pitiful figure, although as readers we do not really pity him. Dorian is not likeable, even before he makes the bargain, and Lord Henry is a strange figure, one who is largely absent from the narrative after the initial scene in the studio. There are also three different tragedies in *Dorian Gray*, realized in the three central characters. The tragedies are interrelated, though there is an odd disconnectedness about the characters' relationships after the first long scene. Basil is the most sympathetic, but it is clear from the outset that, although he is sincere, he is also weak. He tells Henry that he trusts him and Henry simply replies 'What nonsense you talk' (*CW* 26). Basil's tragedy is not that he dies, or that the other characters fail him, or that his love for Dorian is unreciprocated, but the confusion of beauty as an abstract quality with its embodiment in a person, and in a male body. Basil's story is the difficulty of being a true artist. He is placed in relation to the tradition of artists and critics that conform to Pater's Renaissance ideal, and Dorian at one point rehearses the familiar roll-call of Michaelangelo, Winckelmann, Montaigne and Shakespeare in describing Basil.

Of the three, it is Basil alone whose story is the rehearsal of the 'problem in Greek ethics' through the idealization of male beauty, and the difficulty of translating that aesthetic experience into a human and emotional one. The problem for Basil, as it is in the rest of the novel, is the relation of art to life. Basil's difficulty is the intrusion of life into art. He says that, while he was painting Dorian in historical and mythical (mainly Greek) costume, all was manageable, but it is the painting of Dorian in modern dress that produces the fatal portrait. What this does is to translate the ideal of the art object into flesh, into a body that is not the marble body of classical art but the modern body of a real man, and the consequence for Basil is the collapse of the boundaries of art and desire. Dorian is unaware of this until Basil makes his 'strange confession'; Dorian has expressed no reciprocal desire, but his observation of the confession is that there 'seemed to him to be something tragic in a friendship so coloured by romance' (*CW* 91). Indeed there is something tragic, and it is the entry of the (feminine) triviality of romance into what should have been a purely intellectual aesthetic arena. Dorian recognizes Basil's goodness and that goodness as being situated in the noble and intellectual love of the paederastia, but he mistakes it. Basil has seen it for what it is, the slip of idealization into idolatry and the effect that this has on the personality of the artist, and, by extension, his ability to create art. He says to Dorian, 'I was dominated, soul, brain, and power by you' (*CW* 89). Basil is as good a critic as he is an artist, and he sees what is wrong in his own work; he has lost the vital sense of self.

The theme of the danger of domination is persistent in *Dorian Gray*. Lord Henry makes a long speech on the effect of influence, which he describes essentially as the removal of the will from the individual: 'he does not think his natural thoughts or burn with his natural passions.' He asserts that any influence is wrong because 'the aim of life is self-development. To realize one's nature perfectly – that is what each of us is here for' (*CW* 28). What Basil loses is the capacity for individuation, and he loses it through the confusion of love and aesthetics. Art, for Wilde, is never safe, never mere entertainment but a dangerous and strenuous pursuit. For Basil the tragedy is the reverse of Dorian's – the portrait has stepped into life and he cannot manage the reality of flesh and blood. In the Platonic scheme of 'spiritual procreancy' Basil and Dorian are the parents of the 'good' portrait – that is, the one that exists before the wish – but it has been created with a flaw.

The second tragedy is Lord Henry's, and it covers some of the same ground. Henry and Dorian are the parents of the 'bad' portrait, the one whose life begins at the moment of the wish. A similar issue of the effect of domination appears in Henry's deliberate decision to take Dorian over, and to seek to dominate him (*CW* 40). He effectively tries to produce Dorian as a living art object, and Wilde sets up a triangular relationship of art and domination between the three men. Both Basil and Henry are defeated in their endeavours. Lord Henry's tragedy is the failure of his work of art, but Wilde gives us no moment of disillusion in Henry. He never sees the portrait, and he appears to be labouring under an illusion about the true nature of Dorian's life. Henry is a rather reduced figure by the time of his last appearance in the novel: his wife has left him and he describes himself as 'wrinkled, and worn, and yellow' and almost repeats Dorian's original bargain in saying to him, 'I wish I could change places with you' (*CW* 154). Wilde described Henry's punishment as that of the spectator of life, finding 'that those who reject the battle are more deeply wounded than those who take part in it' (*L.* 430). This is another implicit critique of Pater's ideal of the non-participant observer.

For Henry there is nowhere to go; he has dwindled through failure to develop, and his speeches at the end of the novel sound like empty repetitions of those at the beginning, especially in view of what the reader knows about Dorian and the results of Henry's experiment in domination. He rejects self-denial, guilt and conscience, but underestimates the persistence of them all in reality. As the portrait shows, they are experiences that must be recognized as the moments of difference in the dialectic, and their contradictions allowed to exert their energy in order for 'sin' to progress. Not to realize these forces does not mean their annihilation, only their displacement, and Dorian's portrait is the double where all his ignored contradictions are located. In desiring to keep his contradictions separate he has condemned himself, because this means that there will be no change or progress in him. It is not the immorality of his actions that Wilde criticizes, but their emptiness. They are mere sensations because they can lead nowhere without the operations of the critical self upon them.

It is also the portrait that allows the reader to understand Henry's tragedy, which is perhaps the least explicit of the three. Henry has put his philosophy into human form, as Basil has put his flawed Greek ideal into paint. Basil lives, and dies, to see the consequence of his action, but only Dorian and the reader see the consequence of Henry's, and we see that he has been as wrong as Basil. Dorian's relation to art is that he does not attempt to create a work but to become one. He is one, or more precisely two, sketched out by Basil and Henry. His life goes out into the art of the portrait, and he fails in both. He cannot separate art from life, ethics from aesthetics. He becomes a mere seeker after sensation, and is reduced to bodily existence, an illustration of Wilde's assertion of the wasteful and destructive effect of pursuing only sensual pleasures. Wilde realizes in *De Profundis*, as Dorian does not, that seeking beautiful experiences for their own sake can easily and imperceptibly become seeking *any* experiences for their own sake. Again this is an implied criticism of Pater, and echoes Ruskin's concern about Aestheticism, that it would become 'the mere operation of sense'.

Wilde wrote in 1894 that *Dorian Gray* 'contains much of me in it. Basil Hallward is what I think I am: Lord Henry what the world thinks me: Dorian what I would like to be – in other ages, perhaps' (*L.* 585). This is how he saw the novel in 1894, but perhaps he also came to regard the distribution of roles in another light. As I have suggested, it is possible to see *De Profundis* in precisely this sense as a rereading of *Dorian Gray*. Wilde seems to identify his own failure alternately as both Basil's and Dorian's. That for which he deserves punishment and for which he must repent is not same-sex desire but the dereliction of his duty as an artist and critic. He calls his relationship with Douglas 'intellectually degrading' (*CW* 982), coloured, we imagine, by the romance that was fatal to Basil Hallward. He documents every instance of his work being interrupted by Douglas's demands and speaks of the 'absolute ruin' of his art and of his weakness as his crime (*CW* 983). After this loss of his creative self he then loses his critical self. From identification with Basil, Wilde moves to identification with Dorian in his unconsidered indulgence of sensation.

> Desire, at the end, was a malady, or a madness, or both, I grew careless of the lives of others. I took pleasure where it pleased me and passed on. I forgot that every little action of the common day makes or unmakes character, and that therefore what one has done in the secret chamber one has some day to cry aloud on the housetops. (*CW* 1018)

What is also interesting in *De Profundis* is that he reproduces not only the tragedy that circulates around the question of art and morality, but the triple structure. In *De Profundis* there is also a triangular relationship where the trio consists of himself, Douglas and Queensberry, and as in *Dorian Gray* it is the alchemy of the three men that produces tragedy. Douglas dominates Wilde in the same way that Dorian dominates Basil, and in the same way that Lord Henry dominates Dorian, making him unable to measure or judge the progress of his life. The role that is most interesting is that of Queensberry, and the descriptions of his part are what make the sections of *De Profundis* about the relationship with Douglas more than just a reproach to a faithless lover. Queensberry becomes a differently demonic Lord Henry, a figure made inflexible by the single pursuit of exerting his will over another man, driven in Queensberry's case by hatred. That other man is alternately Wilde and Douglas, and Wilde uses of Queensberry exactly the same terminology of domination that he has employed in *Dorian Gray*.

The relationship of three personalities seems to have been meaningful to Wilde. In addition to the identification with all three characters in *Dorian Gray,* he also said that he was 'certain that I have three separate and distinct souls' (E. 133–4). There is yet another set of triple relationships and another dangerous picture in 'The Portrait of Mr W. H.' published in 1889. Like 'Pen, Pencil and Poison', this short story can be seen as a kind of rehearsal of some of the issues in *Dorian Gray*. There is a rather bewildering number of triangles of shifting composition in 'Mr W. H.'. At the core of the story is the relationship narrated in the sonnets themselves, between the writer, the beautiful man to whom they are addressed and the Dark Lady. This trio does not consist of a stable set of characters though; as the interpretation of the sonnets proceeds, the personnel in those roles are continually being changed according to the different theories. Beyond that Elizabethan triangle there is one in the present, consisting of the narrator, Erskine and Cyril Graham. Cyril is dead by the time the narrator hears of him, but his presence and his work are crucial in determining the relationship between the other two. The other absent figure who shifts in and out of the relationships is Shakespeare himself, and at points during the narrator's reading of the sonnets, it is as though the triangle consists of him, Shakespeare and Willie Hughes. Unlike in *Dorian Gray* and *De Profundis,* however, not all of these relationships produce tragedy. Shakespeare is held up as the ideal artist, who 'worshipped one who was the interpreter of his vision, as he was the incarnation of his dreams' (*CW* 324). As we know from the repeated inclusion of Shakespeare's name in the roll-call of the vindications of same-sex desire, he was regarded implicitly by Pater, and much more explicitly by Wilde, as embodying the achievement of the Greek ideal. Wilde writes of the translation of Plato's *Symposium* and insists that Shakespeare both knew it and used it in his work, particularly the 'analogies it draws between intellectual enthusiasm and the physical passion of love, in its dream of the incarnation of the Idea in a beautiful and living form, and of a real spiritual conception with a travail and a bringing to birth'

(*CW* 324). The children that Shakespeare exhorts the young man to have are not children of flesh and blood, but the immortal metaphorical children of the paederastic relationship, works of art. This is the relationship to which the artist should aspire, and whose terrible failure is described in *Dorian Gray* and mourned so painfully in *De Profundis*. The beauty and productivity of Shakespeare's relationship to the 'onlie begetter' of the sonnets are placed in contrast to others in the story. Cyril's death is close to a version of Dorian's. Both are lovely young men with tragically dead parents who are idolized by their friend, and both are involved in the production of flawed portraits. Cyril has the portrait forged to prove the existence of the love that is embedded in the writing, but he says to Erskine, 'I did it purely for your sake' (*CW* 311). Like the tainted artistic offspring of Basil and Dorian, the portrait of Willie Hughes is the flawed child of Erskine and Cyril, made out of obsession, and Cyril dies by suicide, offering his life as a proof of the reality of his idea. The relationship of the narrator with Shakespeare and Hughes almost produces a similar tragedy, as the narrator becomes similarly dominated by the theory. He is saved, however, by the realization of the nature of influence. He says, 'Influence is simply a transference of personality, a mode of giving away what is most precious to one's self, and its exercise produces a sense, and, it may be, a reality of loss' (*CW* 345), and he draws back from the influence of Shakespeare, Hughes and Cyril. The final triangle collapses with the death of Erskine, which, oddly, is also a forgery, this time of a suicide in an attempted replication of Cyril's, and it too is a failed work of art. As the last tragedy is averted, the story ends with the portrait hanging safely, still fascinating but only a reminder of the danger of the loss of self that it represents. This is how Dorian's portrait could have been, had any of the men realized the inevitable trajectory of their actions and ideas, and of the perilous nature of their relations with one another. *De Profundis* suggests that it is, indeed, how Wilde's own life could have been if he had remained true to his critical and artistic philosophy.

Epilogue: Leaving Wilde

Oscar Wilde left Reading prison on the evening of the 18 May 1897. He was taken to Pentonville prison in London and released from there early the next morning. He was met by his friends More Adey and Stewart Headlam, who took him to Headlam's house to wait for the boat train for France. While there he sent a message to a Jesuit community, asking if he could take a six-month retreat with them. His request was refused and he left England that night: he would never return. Wilde crossed the Channel to Dieppe, where he was met by Reggie Turner and Robert Ross, and he handed Ross the manuscript of *De Profundis*.

He was physically much changed by his imprisonment, and there was no question of the possibility of his returning to anything like the social position he had once occupied. It was difficult for him to work, and, although he spoke of other writing, *The Ballad of Reading Gaol* is the only piece he produced after his release. Much of his time was spent in re-editing the texts of the plays and negotiating the sale of their copyright in order to relieve his dire financial situation. He wrote some letters to newspapers on prison reform, but it is hard to see him, as some critics have suggested, as radicalized by his incarceration. *The Ballad of Reading Gaol* is a human response to what he saw and experienced in prison, and it represents similar attitudes to suffering to those shown in the fairy tales. His generosity to the convicts to whom he sent money, and to the warder dismissed for giving biscuits to child prisoners, is no different from the generosity for which he had always been known. His response to the children is even more understandable; he had always despised cruelty and he missed his own sons, whom he was never to see again.

Wilde did become more open, in his letters at least, about his transactions with male prostitutes; but in essence they were no different from his participation in the London sex trade. He was not prompted to any more public discussion of issues of sexuality or to campaign for the repeal of the Labouchère Amendment, even though he notes in the letter to George Ives that this would be the ideal. He writes too of the loneliness he experienced in his exile. Despite his bitter criticisms in *De Profundis*, to the distress of some of his friends, and in danger of losing his small allowance from Constance, he met Douglas again, and the two of them lived together for a few months in Naples. He described it as a refuge from loneliness, but also in fatalistic terms: 'I dare say that what I have done is fatal, but it had to be done. It was necessary that Bosie and I come together again; I saw no other life for myself' (*L.* 950). Douglas had not changed, and when it became clear that he expected Wilde to earn the money to support them both, the abbreviated and muted repetition of their previous times together was over. It seemed that Wilde had realized more clearly, as he had written in *De Profundis*, the nature of their relationship. Douglas no longer dominated Wilde, and when the Marquess of Queensberry died in January 1900, the triangle was finally broken. Although Douglas came into his inheritance, he refused to give Wilde any more than a few pounds.

A certain fatalism marks many of Wilde's letters from the years between his release and his death. Constance died in April 1898 and, after visiting her grave, Wilde wrote to Ross: 'I was deeply affected – with a sense, also, of the uselessness of all regrets. Nothing could have been otherwise, and Life is a very terrible thing' (*L.* 1128). In keeping with the revisiting of his life as a tragedy instead of a comedy, he sees its events as predetermined. At his most pessimistic, as when visiting Constance's grave, he saw his life as wasted, but in the last paragraph of *De Profundis* he writes:

> What lies before me is my past. I have got to make myself look on that with different eyes, to make the world look on it with different

> eyes, to make God look on it with different eyes. This I cannot do by ignoring it, or slighting it, or praising it, or denying it. It is only to be done fully by accepting it as an inevitable part of the evolution of my life and character: by bowing my head to everything that I have suffered. (*CW* 1059)

When at his most determined, he wanted to continue to see his life in terms of evolutionary development and to recuperate the tragedy into a penitential cleansing.

When Wilde died, three years after his release, the contest for his legacy began. For many people, particularly in the years leading up to the First World War, he continued to represent all that was a moral danger to Britain, and there were still legal and social persecutions of those associated with 'the cult of Wilde'. Relations between his friends often turned to open hostility; Douglas began to repudiate Wilde and brought several legal actions in defence of his own reputation. The faithful Robert Ross tried to protect Wilde's literary legacy, and produced an edition of his collected works in 1908. In 1909 Wilde's remains were moved from the small provincial cemetery at Bagneux to Père Lachaise, and marked by Jacob Epstein's impressive modernist monument.

The modernism of the funerary sculpture is in contrast to Wilde's work. In formal terms, Wilde's writing is certainly not innovative; his fictional work has no recognizable relation to the avant-garde of the twentieth century. His poetry can be seen as part of the legacy of post-Romanticism; his drama, with the exception of the Symbolist *Salome*, is in the traditional form of well-made plays. *Dorian Gray* is a Victorian Gothic novella, and the tales are part of the fairy- and folk-tale revival of the later nineteenth century. It is mainly for his non-fictional prose and criticism that the claim for modernity has latterly been made, but, as I have shown, in many ways it was the product of very distinctly nineteenth-century influences. In intellectual terms I think his past always did lie before him, in the shape of his belief in the evolutionary synthesis of Oxford Hegelianism. If that set of ideas had any impact in the twentieth century, it was in the deeply conservative modernism of writers like T. S. Eliot.

It is not only his ideas that have been seen as modern but (and possibly more so) his carefully created self. He was an enthusiastic participant in the burgeoning consumer culture of his period, and this is certainly a culture that came to dominate the twentieth century, but he does not represent any challenge to it. If he is modern in this respect, then again it seems to be a conformist position. His Irishness and his sexuality he saw as aspects of his multiple self, not as defining elements of his existence. The identity politics of the twentieth century that sought to conscript him to a single cause would seem in direct opposition to his faith in dialectical change. Wilde wrote in one of his lectures: 'he who seems to stand most remote from his age is he who mirrors it best, because he has stripped life of what is accidental and transitory' (*EL* 131). When the accidental and transitory are stripped from Wilde, he perhaps stands as the last of the Victorians.

Notes

PROLOGUE. SITUATING WILDE

1. St John Ervine, *Oscar Wilde: A Present Time Appraisal* (London: George Allen & Unwin, 1951), 7.
2. Arthur Ransome, *Oscar Wilde: A Critical Study* (London: Martin Secker, 1912), 20.
3. Graham Robertson in E. H. Mikhail, *Oscar Wilde: Interviews and Recollections*, 2 vols. (London: Macmillan, 1979), i. 213.
4. Merlin Holland and Rupert Hart Davis say in their introduction to the *Complete Letters* that 'no fact, date or statement given by Frank Harris or Lord Alfred Douglas can be accepted without reliable corroborative evidence' (*L.*, p. xvii).
5. Mikhail, *Interviews*, (London: Macmillan, 1979), ii. 424.
6. J. T. Grein, Review, *Sunday Times*, 8 Dec. 1901.
7. Wilde was involved in three trials. In the first, which ran 3–5 April 1895, he was the plaintiff, accusing the Marquess of Queensberry of libel. The prosecution withdrew its case and Queensberry was acquitted. On the evening of 5 April Wilde was arrested and charged with seven counts of gross indecency, and the second trial opened on 26 April. At its close on 29 April the jury could not agree, and a third trial began on 22 May. On 25 May Wilde was sentenced to two years' imprisonment with hard labour.
8. W. L. Leadman, 'The Literary Position of Oscar Wilde', *Westminster Review* (Aug. 1906), 166: 201.
9. For example: *Complete Works* (London: Castle Press, 1948); *Complete Works* (London: Collins, 1966); the full text of *De Profundis*, published privately by Wilde's son Vyvyan in 1949; a collection of essays edited by Hesketh Pearson (London: Methuen, 1950); and the long version of 'The Portrait of Mr W. H.' (London: Methuen, 1958).
10. W. B. Yeats, 'Introduction', in *The Oxford Book of Modern Verse* (Oxford: Oxford University Press, 1936), p. xi.

11. Quoted in Regenia Gagnier, *Idylls of the Marketplace: Oscar Wilde and the Victorian Public*, (Aldershot: Scolar Press, 1987), 146.

CHAPTER 1. MAKING THE SELF

1. John Ruskin, *The Queen of the Air* (London: George Allen, 1898), 141.
2. Walter Pater, *The Renaissance: Studies in Art and Poetry* (Oxford: Oxford University Press, 1986), 150. There is a curious echo of the wording of the Obscene Publications Act of 1857 in Pater's reasoning here, where the act defines obscenity as material tending 'to deprave and corrupt . . . those whose minds are open to such immoral influences and into whose hands it is likely to fall'.
3. Pater, *Renaissance*, 152.
4. Walter Pater, *Marius the Epicurean* (Harmondsworth: Penguin, 1985), 116.
5. See Linda Dowling, *Hellenism and Homosexuality in Victorian Oxford* (Ithaca, NY, and London: Cornell University Press, 1994).
6. Pater, *Marius*, 294–5.
7. Ibid. 293.
8. Pater, *Renaissance*, 153.
9. Charles Darwin, *The Origin of Species* (Harmondsworth: Penguin, 1968), 116.
10. Edwin Ray Lankester, *Degeneration: A Chapter in Darwinism* (London: Macmillan, 1880), 59–60.
11. Max Nordau, *Degeneration*, first published 1895, trans. George L. Mosse (Lincoln, Neb., and London: University of Nebraska Press, 1993), 22.

CHAPTER 2. SELF AND SOCIETY

1. The question of when Wilde first began to have sexual relationships with men is highly contested. Ellmann presents Ross as the first man with whom Wilde had a physical relationship, but others have argued for earlier candidates, as far back as Wilde's preparatory school. This is perhaps not an issue that really matters; Wilde's admiration and love for men are clear throughout his adult life, as is his participation in the network of male prostitution both before and after his imprisonment. There seems little to be gained in attempting to establish a precise date or person for Wilde's first homosexual relationship.
2. Norbert Kohl, *Oscar Wilde: The Works of a Conformist Rebel*, trans. David Henry Wilson (Cambridge: Cambridge University Press, 1989).

3. George Bernard Shaw, 'My Memories of Oscar Wilde', in Frank Harris, *Oscar Wilde: His Life and Confessions*, 2 vols. (New York: Published by the author, 1916), ii. 389.
4. E. H. Mikhail, *Oscar Wilde: Interviews and Recollections*, 2 vols. (London: Macmillan, 1979), i. 62.
5. Shaw, in Harris, *Life and Confessions*, ii. 388.
6. George Bernard Shaw, *Our Theatres in the Nineties* (London: Constable and Co., 1931), 10.
7. E. Mason and R. Ellmann (eds.), *The Critical Writings of James Joyce* (New York: Viking Press, 1959), 203.
8. Declan Kiberd, *Inventing Ireland: The Literature of the Modern Nation* (London: Jonathan Cape, 1995).
9. Richard Pine, *The Thief of Reason: Oscar Wilde and Modern Ireland* (Dublin: Gill & Macmillan, 1995).
10. See e.g. Ulick O'Connor's play, *A Trinity of Two* (1988), which dramatizes the differences between the two men.
11. Laurel Brake, *Subjugated Knowledges: Journalism, Gender and Literature in the Nineteenth Century* (Basingstoke: Macmillan, 1994), 142.
12. Quoted in John Stokes, *In the Nineties* (Hemel Hempstead: Harvester Wheatsheaf, 1989), 14.
13. Sally Ledger, *The New Woman: Fiction and Feminism at the Fin de Siècle* (Manchester: Manchester University Press, 1997), 111.
14. Kerry Powell, *Oscar Wilde and the Theatre of the 1890s* (Cambridge: Cambridge University Press, 1990), 2.
15. Ibid. 13.
16. Joel Kaplan, 'Wilde on the Stage', in Peter Raby (ed.), *The Cambridge Companion to Oscar Wilde* (Cambridge: Cambridge University Press, 1997), 249.
17. See e.g. Bram Djikstra, *Idols of Perversity: Fantasies of Feminine Evil in the Fin de Siècle* (Oxford: Oxford University Press, 1986), which includes a chapter on the various representations of Salome.

CHAPTER 3. SEXUALITY AND THE SELF

1. *National Observer*, 6 Apr. 1895.
2. See Sally Ledger, *The New Woman: Fiction and Feminism at the Fin de Siècle* (Manchester: Manchester University Press, 1997).
3. Alan Sinfield, *The Wilde Century: Effeminacy, Oscar Wilde and the Queer Moment* (London: Cassell, 1994), p. vii.
4. F. B. Smith, 'Labouchère's Amendment to the Criminal Law Amendment Act', *Historical Studies*, 17/6 (Oct. 1976), 165–73.
5. Michel Foucault, *The History of Sexuality* (London: Penguin, 1977), i. 104.

6. Max Nordau, *Degeneration*, first published 1895, trans. George L. Mosse (Lincoln, Neb.: University of Nebraska Press, 1993), 317.
7. Stead wrote to Robert Ross in 1905, thanking him for a copy of *De Profundis*, saying '[I] never joined the herd of his assailants.' Quoted in Karl Beckson (ed.), *Oscar Wilde: The Critical Heritage* (London: Routledge & Kegan Paul, 1970), 242.
8. Foucault, *History*, i. 43.
9. E. M. Forster, *Maurice* (London: Penguin, 2000), 139. This novel was first published in 1971, although Forster's preface states that it was finished in 1914.
10. Havelock Ellis, *Studies in the Psychology of Sex* (New York: F. A. Davis Company 1936), 352.
11. Ed Cohen, *Talk on the Wilde Side: Towards a Genealogy of a Discourse on Male Sexualities* (London: Routledge, 1993), 4.
12. Frank Harris, *Oscar Wilde: His Life and Confessions*, 2 vols. (New York: Published by the author, 1916), ii. 286.
13. Lucy Bland, *Banishing the Beast: English Feminism and Sexual Morality 1885–1914* (Harmondsworth: Penguin, 1995), 288.
14. Quoted in Gary Schmidgall, *The Stranger Wilde* (London: Abacus, 1994), 222.
15. Harris, *Life and Confessions*, i. 106.
16. John Addington Symonds, *A Problem in Greek Ethics* (Privately Published, 1883), 7.
17. Ibid. 8.
18. Ibid. 13.
19. John Addington Symonds, *A Problem in Modern Ethics*, first published privately 1896, repr. in John Lauritsen (ed.), *Male Love* (New York: Pagan Press, 1983), 81.
20. Symonds, *Modern Ethics*, 81.
21. Ibid. 104–5.
22. Letter dated 22 July 1890, in Horatio Brown (ed.), *Letters and Papers of John Addington Symonds* (New York; no publisher, 1923), 240.
23. Wilde's use of the term 'stepmother' here is interesting, as it echoes the phrase 'step-children of nature' used by the sexologist Richard von Krafft-Ebing. His book *Psychopathia Sexualis* was published in German in 1886, and, although it was not translated into English until 1892, ideas from it were in circulation in England before the English publication. Wilde's use of the term suggests at least a familiarity with current terminology, and possibly a knowledge of Krafft-Ebing's work.
24. Stuart Mason (pseudonym of Christopher Millard), *Oscar Wilde: Art and Morality* (London: Frank Palmer, 1907), 22.
25. *Scots Observer*, 5 July 1890, iv. 181.

Select Bibliography

Note: There are many different editions of Wilde's work, some of which give poor versions of the texts. I have given here the first editions in book form and modern scholarly editions.

WORKS BY OSCAR WILDE

As first published in book form

Ravenna (Oxford: Thomas Shrimpton and Sons, 1878).

Vera, Or the Nihilists (London: Ranken & Co., 1880).

Poems (London: David Bogue, 1881).

The Happy Prince and Other Tales, illustrated by Walter Crane and Jacomb Hood (London: David Nutt, 1888).

A House of Pomegranates, illustrated by Charles Ricketts and Charles Shannon (London: Osgood, McIlvaine & Co., 1891).

Intentions (London: Osgood, McIlvaine & Co., 1891).

Lord Arthur Savile's Crime and Other Stories (London: Osgood, McIlvaine & Co., 1891).

The Picture of Dorian Gray (London: Ward Lock & Co., 1891).

Lady Windermere's Fan (London: Elkin Matthews & John Lane, 1893).

Salome in French 1893, in English, with illustrations by Aubrey Beardsley 1894 (London: Elkin Matthews & John Lane).

The Sphinx, illustrated by Charles Ricketts (London: Elkin Matthews & John Lane, 1894).

A Woman of No Importance (London: John Lane, 1894).

The Soul of Man (London: Privately Printed, 1895).

Oscariana (London: Arthur Humphries, 1895).

The Ballad of Reading Gaol (London: Leonard Smithers & Co., 1898).

An Ideal Husband (London: Leonard Smithers & Co., 1899).

The Importance of Being Earnest (London: Leonard Smithers & Co., 1899).

De Profundis (London: Methuen, 1905). Heavily expurgated version. Full text published privately by Wilde's son Vyvyan in 1949.

The Collected Works of Oscar Wilde, ed. Robert Ross, 14 vols. (London: Methuen, 1908).

—— *Essays and Lectures*, (London: Methuen, 1909).

Pearson, Hesketh (ed.), *Essays by Oscar Wilde* (London: Methuen, 1950).

The Portrait of Mr W. H. (New York: Mitchell Kennerley, 1921). Short version. Full version *The Portrait of Mr W. H.* (London: Methuen, 1958).

Modern Editions

The Complete Works of Oscar Wilde, i. *Poems and Poems in Prose*, ed. Karl Beckson and Bobby Fong (Oxford: Oxford University Press, 2000).

Complete Shorter Fiction, ed. Isobel Murray (Oxford: Oxford University Press, 1979).

The Picture of Dorian Gray, ed. Donald Lawler (New York and London: W. W. Norton & Co., 1988).

Lady Windermere's Fan, ed. Ian Small (New York and London: W. W. Norton & Co., 1999).

Salome (London: Faber & Faber, 1989).

A Woman of No Importance, ed. Ian Small (New York and London, W. W. Norton & Co., 1993).

The Soul of Man Under Socialism and Selected Critical Prose, ed. Linda Dowling (London: Penguin, 2001).

An Ideal Husband, ed. Russell Jackson (New York and London: W. W. Norton & Co., 1993).

The Importance of Being Earnest, ed. Russell Jackson (New York and London: W. W. Norton & Co., 1980).

De Profundis and Other Writings, ed. Hesketh Pearson (Harmondsworth: Penguin, 1984).

Collins Complete Works of Oscar Wilde, (Glasgow: Harper Collins, 2003).

BIOGRAPHY

Ellmann, Richard, *Oscar Wilde* (London: Hamish Hamilton, 1987; reissued Harmondsworth: Penguin, 1988). This is the standard biography.

Harris, Frank, *Oscar Wilde: His Life and Confessions*, 2 vols. (New York: Published by the author, 1916). Personal recollections by the author and conversations with others who knew Wilde. The veracity of Harris has frequently been questioned.

Holland, Merlin, *Irish Peacock & Scarlet Marquess: The Real Trial of Oscar Wilde* (London: Fourth Estate, 2003). Complete transcript of the first trial with introduction.

—— and Hart-Davis, Rupert, *The Complete Letters of Oscar Wilde* (London: Fourth Estate, 2000). There are many editions of Wilde's letters; this is the most complete to date.

Hyde, H. Montgomery, *Oscar Wilde: A Biography*, first published 1975 (London: Penguin, 2001). Important biography that was standard until the publication of Ellmann's.

—— *The Trials Of Oscar Wilde* (New York, Dover, 1973). First published in 1948. No transcripts of the trials were thought to exist until the publication of Holland. This is a reconstruction from notes, newspaper accounts and recollections.

McKenna, Neil, *The Secret Life of Oscar Wilde* (London: Century 2003). Sexual and emotional biography, presenting new material and witness statements from the trials. Argues that Wilde's sexuality is the only way to understand his work.

Mikhail, E. H. (ed.), *Oscar Wilde: Interviews and Recollections*, 2 vols. (London: Macmillan, 1979). A large collection of anecdotes and reminiscences of those who knew Wilde.

Pearson, Hesketh, *The Life of Oscar Wilde* (London: Methuen, 1946). First significant biography.

Smith, Philip E., and Helfand, Michael S. (eds.), *Oscar Wilde's Oxford Notebooks: A Portrait of a Mind in the Making* (Oxford: Oxford University Press, 1989). Personal notes kept by Wilde during his undergraduate years with commentary by the editors on his sources and influences.

CRITICAL WORKS

Note: The critical literature on Wilde is extensive. For a comprehensive bibliography see Ian Small, *Oscar Wilde Revalued: An Essay on New Materials and Methods of Research* (Greensboro, NC: ELT Press, 1993) and *Oscar Wilde: Recent Research: A Supplement to 'Oscar Wilde Revalued'* (Greensboro, NC: ELT Press, 2000).

Bartlett, Neil, *Who Was That Man? A Present for Mr Oscar Wilde* (London: Serpent's Tail, 1988). An inventive subjective and critical reflection on Wilde, his contemporary society and his legacy.

Bashford, Bruce, *The Critic as Humanist* (London: Fairleigh Dickinson University Press, 1999). Argues for the importance of Wilde as a critical thinker, not only in the essays but throughout his work.

Beckson, Karl (ed.), *Oscar Wilde: The Critical Heritage* (London: Routledge & Kegan Paul, 1970). An anthology of critical responses to the works, from early reviews and correspondence to assessments in the 1960s.

Behrendt, Patricia Flanagan, *Oscar Wilde: Eros and Aesthetics* (London: Macmillan, 1991). Relates Wilde's sexuality to his aesthetic development, with the figure of Eros as representing the loss of control through love.

Bloom, Harold (ed.), *Oscar Wilde: Modern Critical Views* (New York: Chelsea House, 2000).

Brake, Laurel, *Subjugated Knowledges: Journalism, Gender and Literature in the Nineteenth Century* (Basingstoke: Macmillan, 1994). Chapter discussing Wilde's editorship of the *Woman's World* and its relationship to women and feminism.

Bristow, Joseph (ed.), *Wilde Writings* (Toronto: University of Toronto Press, 2003). Good collection of critical essays on different aspects of Wilde's work and its contexts.

—— 'Wilde's Fatal Effeminacy', in his *Effeminate England: Homoerotic Writing after 1885* (Buckingham: Open University Press, 1995).

—— 'Wilde, *Dorian Gray* and Gross Indecency', in his (ed.), *Sexual Sameness* (London: Routledge, 1992).

Brown, Julia Prewett, *Cosmopolitan Criticism: Oscar Wilde's Philosophy of Art* (Charlottesville, Va.: University of Virginia Press, 1997). Biographical reading of the work in the context of nineteenth-century European philosophy.

Coakley, Davis, *Oscar Wilde: The Importance of Being Irish* (Dublin: Town House, 1994). Explores the impact on Wilde of his upbringing in Ireland, the cultural life of late-nineteenth-century Dublin and the Irish American experiences of his US tour.

Cohen, Ed, *Talk on the Wilde Side: Towards a Genealogy of a Discourse on Male Sexualities* (London: Routledge, 1993). Discusses the language used in the trials and their reporting to show how modern ideas of sexuality crystallized around Wilde.

Danson, Lawrence, *Wilde's Intentions: The Artist in his Criticism* (Oxford: Clarendon Press, 1997). Focuses on *Intentions*, with a chapter on each essay. It discusses the texts' original reception, and suggests that paradox and antagonistic discourses are synthesized by Wilde's language.

Dellamora, Richard, 'Oscar Wilde, Social Purity, and *An Ideal Husband*', *Modern Drama*, 37 (1994), 120–38.

Dowling, Linda, *Hellenism and Homosexuality in Victorian Oxford* (Ithaca, NY, and London: Cornell University Press, 1994).

—— *Language and Decadence in the Victorian Fin de Siècle* (Princeton: Princeton University Press, 1986).

Doylen, Michael R., 'Oscar Wilde's *De Profundis*: Homosexual Self-Fashioning on the Other Side of Scandal', *Victorian Literature and Culture*, 27 (1999), 547–66.

Eltis, Sos, *Revising Wilde: Society and Subversion in the Plays of Oscar Wilde* (Oxford: Clarendon Press, 1996). Concentrates on anarchism, feminism and socialism in the dramas; locates Wilde as a genuine radical and harsh critic of late-nineteenth-century society.

Ervine, St John, *Oscar Wilde: A Present Time Appraisal* (London: George Allen & Unwin, 1951). Semi-biographical attempt to consider Wilde's work in critical terms.

Foldy, Michael S., *The Trials of Oscar Wilde: Deviance, Morality and Late-Victorian Society* (New Haven: Yale University Press, 1997). Examines the cultural context of the trials and describes the climate of opinion established by the press that helped to secure a conviction.

Frankel, Nick, 'Ave Imperiatrix: Oscar Wilde and the Poetry of Englishness', *Victorian Poetry*, 35 (1997), 117–37.

Gagnier, Regenia, *Idylls of the Marketplace: Oscar Wilde and the Victorian Public* (Aldershot: Scolar Press, 1987). Important and influential study of Wilde in the context of commodity and commerce. Argues that he presents a critique of social superficiality and commodity fetishism, but that his views on freedom are compromised by his own participation in consumer culture.

—— (ed.), *Critical Essays on Oscar Wilde* (New York: G. K. Hall, 1992). Good collection of essays; reprints Christopher Craft, 'Alias Bunbury', important essay on coded language in *The Importance of Being Earnest*.

Gillespie, Michael Patrick, *Oscar Wilde and the Poetics of Ambiguity* (Gainesville, Fla.: Gainesville University Press of Florida, 1996). Argues that the work actively promotes multiple interpretations and it is important not to attempt to simplify that multiplicity. Useful section on the relations between text and illustration in *Salome*.

Guy, Josephine M., 'Oscar Wilde: Traditional Iconoclast', in her *The British Avant-Garde: The Theory and Politics of Tradition* (Hemel Hempstead: Harvester Wheatsheaf, 1991).

—— and Small, Ian, *Oscar Wilde's Profession: Writing and the Culture Industry in the Late Nineteenth Century* (Oxford: Oxford University Press, 2000). Sees Wilde as a professional writer heavily concerned with self-promotion. Reinterprets his plagiarism and self-plagiarism as responses to the demands of the marketplace.

Kaplan, Joel (ed.), *Modern Drama*, 37 (1994). Special issue devoted to Wilde.

Kiberd, Declan, *Inventing Ireland: The Literature of the Modern Nation* (London: Jonathan Cape, 1995). Identifies Wilde as the first writer of modern Ireland and a determined anti-colonialist. Devotes much attention to the fairy tales and discusses their political effect.

Knox, Melissa, *Oscar Wilde: A Long and Lovely Suicide* (New Haven and London: Yale University Press, 1994). Controversial study that relies on the contested thesis that Wilde had syphilis to produce a psychoanalytic reading of the works.

Kohl, Norbert, *Oscar Wilde: The Works of a Conformist Rebel*, trans. David Henry Wilson (Cambridge: Cambridge University Press, 1988). Takes the view that Wilde adopts the posture of rebellion, but that he is more accurately identified as a conservative liberal aesthete.

Mason, Stuart (pseudonym of Christopher Millard), *Oscar Wilde: Art and Morality* (London: Frank Palmer, 1907). One of the first efforts to secure a literary legacy for Wilde.

McCormack, Jerusha (ed.), *Wilde the Irishman* (New Haven and London: Yale University Press, 1998). A collection of responses to Wilde and his work from poets, actors, playwrights and novelists, as well as literary critics.

Nassaar, Christopher, *Into the Demon Universe: A Literary Exploration of Oscar Wilde* (New Haven: Yale University Press, 1974). One of the first full-length critical studies. Dismisses the poetry as second rate, but sees Wilde as a late Romantic, influenced by their ideas on the demonic impulse to sin and crime.

Nunokawa, Jeff, *Oscar Wilde* (New York: Chelsea House, 1994).

—— 'The Importance of Being Bored: The Dividends of Ennui in *The Picture of Dorian Gray*', *Studies in the Novel*, 28 (1996), 357–75.

Pine, Richard, *The Thief of Reason: Oscar Wilde and Modern Ireland* (Dublin: Gill & Macmillan, 1995). Proposes that Wilde's Irishness enabled him to conceptualize an 'in-between' existence, a kind of third space, which is reflected in his writings. Pine also argues strongly for Wilde's strong influence on Modernism.

Powell, Kerry, *Oscar Wilde and the Theatre of the 1890s* (Cambridge: Cambridge University Press, 1990). Detailed study of the world of 1890s theatre; explores a number of forgotten contemporary plays and points out how Wilde's society comedies are deeply indebted to the prevailing style of those other works.

Price, Jody, *'A Map of Utopia': Oscar Wilde's Theory for Social Transformation* (New York: Peter Lang, 1996).

Raby, Peter, *Oscar Wilde* (Cambridge: Cambridge University Press, 1990). Introductory account of the life and work.

—— (ed.), *The Cambridge Companion to Oscar Wilde* (Cambridge: Cambridge University Press, 1997). Collection of critical essays that covers most of the range of Wilde's work.

Ransome, Arthur, *Oscar Wilde: A Critical Study*, (London: Martin Secker, 1912) Early attempt to separate Wilde's work from his controversial reputation.

Roditi, Edouard, *Oscar Wilde* (Norfolk, CO.: New Direction Books, 1947). Along with Ervine, Pearson and Woodcock, part of mid-twentieth-century efforts to bring Wilde into serious literary consideration.

Roden, Frederick S. (ed.), *Advances in Oscar Wilde Studies* (Basingstoke: Macmillan, 2004). Collection of essays summarizing recent critical opinions.

Sammells, Neil, *Wilde Style: The Plays and Prose of Oscar Wilde* (London: Longman, 2000). Deals with the drama, fiction and non-fiction to explore the importance of the idea of style. Relates style to modernity. Final chapter examines Wilde's influence on popular culture in recent years.

Sandalescu, C. George (ed.), *Rediscovering Oscar Wilde* (Gerrards Cross: Colin Smythe, 1994). Wide-ranging collection of critical essays derived from major international conference.

Shewan, Rodney, *Oscar Wilde: Art and Egotism* (London: Macmillan, 1977).

Sinfield, Alan, *The Wilde Century: Effeminacy, Oscar Wilde and the Queer Moment* (London: Cassell, 1994). Examines discourses of gender and sexuality preceding Wilde; outlines how these changed at the time of the trials, and Wilde's legacy in twentieth-century gay and queer theory.

Sloan, John, *Oscar Wilde* (Oxford: Oxford University Press, 2003). Places Wilde's work in the context of late-nineteenth-century social and intellectual issues. Also includes a chapter on the film, television and stage productions of Wilde's works.

Stokes, John, *Oscar Wilde: Myths, Miracles and Imitations* (Cambridge: Cambridge University Press, 1996). Uses Wilde as a connecting link between a group of essays on *fin de siècle* phenomena.

Tanitch, Robert, *Oscar Wilde on Stage and Screen* (London: Methuen, 1999).

Willoughby, Guy, *Art and Christhood: The Aesthetics of Oscar Wilde* (London: Associated University Presses, 1993). Suggests that the figure of Jesus can provide a means of seeing Wilde's work as a coherent whole, and that Wilde's Christ is an idealized version of himself.

Varty, Anne, *A Preface to Oscar Wilde* (Harlow: Longman, 1998.) Very good brief introduction.

Woodcock, George, *The Paradox of Oscar Wilde* (London and New York: T. V. Boardman and Co., 1949). One of a small group of post-war critical and biographical books beginning to re-establish Wilde as a serious writer and critic.

Worth, Katharine, *Oscar Wilde* (London: Macmillan, 1983). Emphasizes the radical aspects of the dramas. Concludes that they are deeply undermining of Victorian hierarchical values, and that Wilde's radical sympathies are expressed through his portrayals of women.

Index